Return from the Dead

THE HISTORY OF GHOSTS, VAMPIRES, WEREWOLVES, AND POLTERGEISTS

DOUGLAS HILL

MACDONALD UNIT 75

SBN 356 03463 1

© Douglas Hill, 1970

First published in 1970 by
Macdonald Unit 75
St Giles House, 49 Poland Street, London, W.1

Made and printed in Great Britain by
Hazell Watson & Viney Ltd, Aylesbury, Bucks

Contents

I
Walking Corpses

I

Walking Corpses

MAN'S ancient and permanent fear of the dead arises, obviously, from his belief that the dead can return. And this belief, in its most basic form, implies the fear that the actual corpse will become reanimated, will somehow force its way through the earth above its grave or past the stone slabs of its tomb, and walk abroad, mouldering and terrible in its winding sheet.

Naturally, such revenants are in the minority when compared with the more usual non-corporeal ghost. But primitive peoples, caring nothing for the fine distinctions of civilisation, have never been troubled by the question whether the ghosts they fear are revived corpses or disembodied spirits. In an old ritual designed to placate the dead, Congolese tribesmen poured food and drink down a channel in the grave-soil right to the corpse's mouth. Were they feeding the body to keep it quiet, or to appease the wandering shade? To the primitive, the question would not arise. The body *is* the soul – in the mystic, symbolic way that a totem object is dedicated to a spirit but also somehow contains the spirit. Or in the way that a masked witchdoctor represents a god but somehow also becomes the god. It is a mystical one-ness not readily grasped by civilised minds that prefer ideas pre-sliced, to fit into separate compartments.

Anyway, in much primitive lore corpses were said to walk, and strong precautions were taken against the event.

Prehistoric bones are still found with indications that the bodies had been tied down; the Oraons of India, among others, pegged the body down, the Chiriguonos of South America buried a corpse head downwards. More practically, some African tribes preferred to maim or dismember corpses to immobilise them, though some pygmy peoples merely cut off the deceased's hair, a traditional source of magical strength.

Not that these preventatives always worked – or else there should not be so many legends of perambulating corpses, primitive or otherwise. Pre-Buddhist Tibetan peoples believed in such resurrections, adding that the mere touch of such a being was fatal. Arab tribesmen believed that a corpse might actively and forcibly resist being taken to its grave. And among North American Indian corpse legends, there is a poignant Plains Indian tale of a young mother, accidentally drowned, whose body returns from the water to suckle the orphaned child.

Supernatural traditions in Brittany do not always separate the returned ghost from its body, and the active corpses there, according to Anatole le Braz, are called the Anaun – the souls. Also from France, in the 4th century, comes a romantic, melodramatic legend of a married couple who died before their love could be consummated. The husband's corpse was later found to have left its tomb, and to have joined the wife in her separate grave.

Greek island lore holds many accounts of restless corpses, with the addition that they are sometimes falsely animated, by devils. Perhaps that explanation accounts for the evil 18th-century British lord, well dead, who rose up from his coffin in a Westmorland church to frighten the parson praying over him. But it is devilry, not devils, that animates all those Irish corpses who in legends leap out of their coffins to join in the apparently irresistible festivities of the wake.

The ancient Egyptians, more death-oriented than most

of the early civilisations, seemed like primitives to reject any distinction between eternal life for the body or for the soul. Certainly they went to enormous trouble to preserve the bodies of deceased aristocrats and kings, and so it is not surprising that some legends come down to us of reanimated mummies. Modern horror fiction has associated Egyptian tombs with dire curses on archaeological desecrators – and indeed even today there have been suggestions that something dark and mysterious lay behind the deaths of people connected with the opening of the tomb of Tutankhamen. British Museum employees were frightened some years ago by the remains of a priestess of Amen-Ra – who apparently rose up now and then, made eerie hammering and sobbing noises from within her mummy case, and visited unpleasant punishments on those who handled the case with disrespect.

But reanimated mummies were not always malevolent – at least, not when in their proper place. A 3rd-century BC Egyptian priest named Khamuas, searching tombs for the god Thoth's great book of magic, held many useful and enjoyable conversations with the dead. And a Coptic bishop of the 6th century AD also talked with mummies in a tomb, according to legend; they told him bloodcurdling tales of their miseries in the afterworld, and he comforted them with Christian reassurances.

Not all cultures preserve their dead as devotedly as did the Egyptians, so it was no wonder that some of legends' reactivated corpses emerge as mere skeletons. Because traditionally the figure of Death is pictured as a skeleton, these fleshless revenants have come to be taken as harbingers of death. Elliott O'Donnell, a tireless British gatherer of ghost lore, offers an account of a girl walking in her garden on All Hallows Eve, hearing footsteps behind, and turning to find herself facing a skeleton dressed identically with herself. According to O'Donnell, she died within the year.

Skeletons play soundless music, an American legend says, on the spectral funeral train of Abraham Lincoln (which will be reintroduced in Chapter Six). Skeletal crews man phantom ships, according to some of the reports of the *Flying Dutchman* and its ilk. And in Brittany an old legend describes a demonic skeleton patrolling the countryside in a cart, summoning those who are about to die.

Nor need the active bones be complete. The skull of a dissolute 17th-century nobleman was said to haunt a stately home in Lancashire, in spite of many attempts to destroy it. And another British house, in Dorset, was the home of a screaming skull – which not only shrieked if it was removed from its shelf, but had the supernatural power also to cause the death of the remover. Several other skulls were in the past kept in British homes out of fear of their power – if they were moved – to visit catastrophe (failed crops, dead livestock and the like) on the house and lands.

The mobile corpses of folklore have not all arisen of their own accord: some have been called up, by living men. One thinks immediately of Mary Shelley's *Frankenstein*, and its film dilutions, wherein an obsessed scientist combines portions of various human cadavers and literally galvanises the resulting creature into life. Fact approached fiction, it seems, when a 19th-century French doctor pumped fresh blood into the head of a guillotined criminal, and claimed that the head regained a lifelike appearance and an expression of 'trouble and amazement' came over the face. Early in the 20th century a pair of occultists in California not only claimed to have discovered the Philosophers' Stone of alchemy (sought primarily as an Elixir of Life), but to have restored a dead woman to life with it.

But then with alchemy we enter areas of magic, and

magic – in the form of necromancy – enlivens rather more corpses, according to the tales, than science or even pseudo-science. Since ancient Mesopotamia, every run-of-the-mill magician has had some expertise in necromancy – which means, as the suffix indicates, divination by means of the dead. Of course, the ancient texts are not always clear whether the bodiless *spirits* of the dead are being called up or whether they are being reinstalled into the actual dead bodies. In Homer, Odysseus summons the dead seer Tiresias to foretell the future, and modern readers tend to see it as the shade of the seer which returns. So, too, spirits were conjured up by the famous Elizabethan occultist Dr Dee, and his associate Edward Kelley – although it is said that these Elizabethans once also awakened a newly dead corpse and talked with it. (Eric Maple, the British writer, comments that Kelley was a well-known ventriloquist, which 'no doubt had a considerable bearing on the success of this operation'.)

The grisly means by which necromancers set out to revive a corpse are fairly well documented. They wear grave clothes taken from other cadavers, they draw magic circles round the coffin at midnight and speak involved incantations. In the end, the spirit returns to the corpse, which answers the necromancer's questions (about the future) in a faint and hollow voice. But sometimes mere fortune-telling or prophecy is not the magician's purpose. He is seeking a willing and a terrifying slave, to do his bidding.

When the revived corpse becomes a sorcerer's slave, it falls into the category of the *zombi*, a word which comes – along with the bulk of zombi lore – from the magic-obsessed and fear-drenched island of Haiti. W. B. Seabrook, an American journalist and travel writer, defines the zombi as 'a soulless human corpse, still dead, but taken from the grave and endowed by sorcery with a mechanical semblance of life'. He describes how Haitians will guard the grave of a loved one until the corpse has certainly begun to decompose – because the zombi masters will not revive a rotting cadaver. And he describes how he was taken (in the 1920s) by a Haitian to see zombis for himself.

In fact, he saw men at work in the canefields, dull, plodding, unresponsive, with 'the eyes of a dead man, not blind, but staring, unfocused, unseeing'. Later he found a semi-rational explanation for what he saw, and for the legend in general: that the evil 'sorcerers' might administer a drug to someone that throws him into a coma, which is mistaken for death. After the burial, the evil-doers revive the man, but keep his mind blanked by other drugs.

The explanation may seem almost as far-fetched as the superstition. At the least, it seems an extraordinarily complicated way to acquire cheap labour for the fields. Nevertheless there is special provision, according to Seabrook, in the Haitian Penal Code against the inducing of such comas, which are termed murder if the recipient is actually buried as if dead.

At any rate, folklore embellishes the notion, as it always will. The sorcerers are believed to revive corpses by a magical incantation employing the dead man's name (the magical potency of names is a well-known motif in supernatural matters). The zombis are never allowed to eat salt, or meat, for either food would restore their awareness – whereupon they would realise they were dead, and would irresistibly seek their graves.

African lore has something of a counterpart, in the *wengwa* of Gabon – a reanimated corpse, sometimes rising of its own volition, sometimes described as having only one eye in the centre of its forehead. In other Gabon legends the wengwa is a corpse by day and a were-leopard by night. In Surinam, sorcerers are supposed to be able to capture people's souls, to be used either to reanimate corpses, or to animate synthetic human bodies fabricated by the magician out of flesh and wood. The latter are called *bakrus,* and are the sorcerer's willing and evil slaves.

Then there is the dancing corpse or *rolang* of Tibetan magical lore, reanimated by a particularly gruesome ritual. The sorcerer lies on the corpse, mouth to mouth, concentrating fiercely on his magical incantation. As it takes effect, the corpse will rise and thresh about, trying to dislodge the sorcerer – and if it did so it would kill him. The sorcerer must cling tightly, and maintain his concentration – until finally the corpse's tongue protrudes. The sorcerer seizes the tongue in his mouth and bites it off; the corpse then collapses, and the sorcerer keeps the tongue as an item of highly potent magic.

None of these cousins to the zombi have caught the popular imagination so much as the Haitian product. And because of this, a note of warning is needed to counter the sensationalised image of Haitian voodoo. It is not solely or even primarily a steamy and primitive collation of orgies and black magic. It is a strikingly complex and often rather beautiful *religion,* with roots in African worship, with elements of ancestor worship and the gentle arts of herbalism combining with ecstatic (but rarely orgiastic) ceremonial worship of ancient gods. Evil magic, voodoo dolls, zombis and the rest are merely the dark side, the superstitious, old-wives'-tales side, of this religion – in the way that 16th-century witchcraft was the dark side of Christianity. The parallel is valid, since both dark sides were largely fictitious, folklorish, wildly exaggerated by sensation-mongers.

There is one more manifestation of the living dead, not yet mentioned, that is equally fictitious and folklorish – and that far outshines the zombi as a favourite among fans of the macabre. It is the vampire – so prominent among revenants, so productive of legends and sublegends, that it deserves a chapter to itself.

2

Blood, Sex, and Vampires

2

Blood, Sex, and Vampires

LIKE the zombi, the vampire is a legendary reanimated corpse. Also like the zombi, the vampire was once a fairly localised legend. Of course, antecedents and distant relatives, similar in a few details, exist in the folklore of many peoples and many ages; and it has had a number of off-shoots among peoples in proximity to its home locality. But in spite of these parallels and correspondences, the vampire itself was originally a Slavonic monster, throwing its shadow over the superstitious in eastern Europe – Hungary, Czechoslovakia, Rumania, the Balkan countries, and their immediate neighbours.

Even the word 'vampire' is an adaptation of the Magyar word *vampir*, which in turn is the same as the Bulgarian *vapir*, Russian *upuir*, and so on. Folklorists believe that the legend of the vampire had not crystallised all its elements, nor built up its notoriety within the Balkan peninsula, much before the 16th century. By the 17th century, a considerable spate of vampire activity seemed to have been stirring in the Balkans: eerie tales and horrified reports and rumours mushroomed.

Also in the 17th century the legend began to spread. A Greek writer, Leone Allacci, produced a slim volume about the vampire belief; other travellers picked up hints of it during passages through eastern Europe, and a few learned churchmen alluded to stories of such creatures reported to them by parishioners. (Naturally they put a diabolical interpretation onto the vampire, not strictly accurate.) Then, in France, a learned Benedictine monk named Dom Augustin Calmet published a full-fledged treatise on ghosts and vampires, in 1746, and the legend thrust itself firmly into the horror lore of the western world.

But if the Slavic conception of the vampire is the main thread in the weave of the legend as we know it, two subsidiary threads must also be noted. First, the antecedents and offshoots – and among the former are some basic beliefs among primitives of the malefic nature of the dead, and the tendency of corpses to rise again, already looked at in Chapter One. These ideas are fundamental contributions to vampire concepts – as is the equally deep-rooted primitive belief about the supernatural power in blood. No one needs reminding of the widespread use of 'blood sacrifice' in primitive invocations of gods; but it could summon lesser spirits too, thanks to its paramount power of life-giving. Many primitive tribes – cannibals, of course, but also some North American Indians – ceremonially drank the blood of slain enemies who had died courageously, to infuse that courage into themselves. For other primitives, consuming any blood was outright taboo – a grievous sin. Blood gives life, blood – as the Bible says – *is* life, in ancient magical belief and symbolism.

So, obviously, it is a short step to the role of blood as a revivifying force. The vampiric corpse spontaneously rises (as opposed to the zombis and their ilk, summoned and empowered by evil magic) and to maintain its 'life in death' it goes in search of sustenance, in the form of the basic stuff of life. Behind this idea lie many more ancient tales of blood-sucking horrors – not revived corpses, but nonetheless the immediate ancestors of the vampire. Like the corpse-eating ghouls of old Arabic legends, who sometimes attacked the living and drank their blood; like the spirits in Homer's *Odyssey*, restored to human awareness by ingesting blood; like the *Lamia* of ancient Rome, vicious female ghosts or demons who enticed men and then devoured them, or sucked their blood. (Other sexually enticing demonic beings, like the incubus and succubus of early Christian demonology, were only rarely believed to consume the flesh or blood of their victims, and so must be considered more distant relatives of the vampire.)

As for the offshoots, more or less contemporary with the burst of vampire lore in the Balkans, they can be especially found in the *vrykolakas* of Greece, generally thought to derive a good deal from Slavonic legend, with all the usual aspects of resuscitated corpses, blood-sucking, and the rest. Parts of Russia far removed from eastern Europe also had tales of vampiric creatures, probably another folklore borrowing from the legend as it occurred in the Ukraine and Poland. These offshoots existed and thrived along with the root legends in the Balkan peninsula, long before the legend began its rapid seeping into western Europe and Britain – though according to Montague Summers, who remains the greatest if not the only authority on vampire lore, the ancient Irish had conceived of a bloodsucking demon called the Dearg-dul, a rather isolated antecedent.

The arrival of the vampire legend in western Europe was achieved partly by the dissemination of Balkan folk tales, but the process was completed by another important secondary thread in the build-up of the legend: pure fiction. Late 18th-century German romanticism found useful fuel in folklore horrors, and the use of the vampire motif in, say, poems by Goethe stimulated further spread of the folk materials. A vampire appears in a poem by Lord Byron, and in another by Southey, fairly early in the 19th century's English romantic tradition – though, oddly, none of the earliest writers of 'Gothic' horror fiction (such as Monk Lewis) brought in vampirism as one of their eerie effects. Other prose writers tossed off more or less derivative attempts at vampire stories – among them, Dr Polidori, that somewhat silly associate of Shelley and Byron who had the effrontery to sign Byron's name to his story. The story produced something of a sensation, and in an indirect way spawned a fad for vampires in Britain and France. In Paris a vampire play was the most talked-about hit in the theatre of the 1820s.

Decades passed without the fad diminishing: Alexandre Dumas wrote his vampire play in the 1850s and it, too, drew packed houses, but before that other dramatic imitators had utilised the motif all across Europe, including a German opera in 1828. (For that matter, Montague Summers mentions vampire plays being staged in London in 1872 and 1909.) The 19th-century French poet, Gautier, used the theme in a major poem, and it occurs too in a dark demonic poem by Baudelaire. Then, in 1847, the whole vampire craze came to a head (though some would see it as a trough rather than a crest) in a 'penny-dreadful' novel by one Thomas Preskett Prest, entitled *Varney the Vampire*. Though more than 800 pages long, this simple, fast-moving, low-brow horror story became an instant bestseller on every level of readership. Vampires, clearly, had come to stay.

Their permanence was assured at the end of the 19th century, when an Irish author named Bram Stoker created the second most famous character of horror fiction after Frankenstein's monster. Stoker's *Dracula* has become a virtual synonym for the vampire; if the ordinary person knows anything about the vampire legend in folklore, he has learned it through the bits of authentic lore that Stoker used – and the considerably fewer bits that were retained in various film versions of Dracula. Yet Stoker studied Balkan folklore while writing his masterpiece – rather more thoroughly than some of the other writers who used the theme. So it would need a detailed analysis of the novel to distinguish between original Balkan folk materials, dressed-up folklore from elsewhere, and Stoker's own imaginative additions. Today, all these elements have come to be jumbled up in a popular conception of vampires which means that there has been a rather striking feedback: folklore has lent itself to fiction which in turn has altered folklore.

Nonetheless, with or without Dracula as a prime example, the nature and habits of the vampire, as legend depicts him, can be outlined. But it will not be the localised, Balkanised vampire that will be described. Since the 19th-century fad ran its course, the vampire has left his narrow and parochial place of origin. He has become a citizen of the world, as much as the ghost or the werewolf have always been.

The vampire's appearance, in the old tales, clearly indicate his 'living dead' nature. Above all, he is invariably lean and cadaverous (because he *is* a cadaver): sometimes leathery and skeletal like a long-dead corpse, but more often merely gaunt. A few of the oldest Slavonic tales picture him stalking about in the shroud or winding sheet, but otherwise he dresses normally – or nearly normally. Count Dracula wore black and only black, an effectively funereal touch.

The well-fed, replete vampire is sometimes said to be horribly bloated or swollen with blood (an image presumably borrowed from the leech). But at other times the nature of his diet is indicated only by the thick ruddiness of his lips – which draw back frequently in a feral snarl to reveal long, sharp, canine teeth. His skin is white with the pallor of death, and in most cases he is icy cold to the touch, though again a full meal might raise his temperature to fever point. His eyes gleam, and sometimes flash red; his hands are exceptionally hairy, even on the palms; his eyebrows are sometimes said to meet above the nose;

his fingernails are curved and clawed; his ears may be pointed as Dracula's were. His breath is fetid, like any carnivore's; and he is preternaturally strong. Remember that Dracula was able to climb down a stone castle wall, head *downwards*, using the strength of his hands and feet alone.

A few odd additions to this list of features are worth including – like the Bulgarian notion that a vampire has only one nostril, or the old Polish idea that his tongue has a sharp point or barb. (Interestingly, the tongue of a vampire bat has such a barb, though it is unlikely that many old wives in Poland knew that fact – or had ever heard of the vampire bat.) In Greece, vampires were said to have blue eyes – which was a roundabout way of saying that people with blue eyes, very rare in Greece until the tourist trade built up, were probably vampires. But then people who were 'different' in some way were always being accused of vampirism, or witchcraft, or the like. At one time or another people with hare-lips, or red hair, or odd birthmarks, or children born with teeth, have all been persecuted as alleged vampires.

The living corpse that is the vampire seems permanently attached to his burial place : one of the many 'rules' that seem to govern his activities is his need to return to his grave, or coffin, or tomb, before daylight every morning, and to sleep in it during the day. Hollywood, with its need for melodramatic climaxes, would have us believe in the old Dracula films that daylight can *destroy* a vampire – but folklore says nothing of the kind. Indeed, some Balkan tales have vampires wandering about freely under the sun. But most of the creatures remain nocturnal in their habits. This fact, plus the added rule (emphasised by Stoker) that the vampire must spend the days in his own coffin, not in any old hideaway, put the creature very much at the mercy of the living vampire hunters.

But then, when it is up and about, the vampire corrects

the balance with quite a few impressive magical powers –
not the least of which is its ability, in many tales, to get in
and out of a grave through six feet of soil. Some old Slav
stories tell of graves punctured by several small holes,
which are channels reaching down to the corpse; the vampire apparently filters up through these – which seems
not much simpler than filtering up through the porous
earth itself. But here again is an example of the old unwillingness to bother with distinctions between corpse and
ghost. The vampire is a material corpse with some of the
powers of an immaterial spirit, and no one in the old days
saw any contradiction. Hungarian tales get round the
problem, though, by giving the vampire the supernatural
ability to change into a cloud or mist. Stoker used this
trick, as he uses the Balkan belief that vampires can control certain fearsome or unpleasant animals – wolves, for
instance, sometimes cats, or rats, even flies.

Occasionally a few tales will give the vampire himself
the power of metamorphosing into an animal. This idea is
probably an overspill from ancient witch tales and equally
ancient werewolf themes. In Rumania, for instance, werewolves are believed to return automatically after death as
vampires – and vampires can often turn themselves into
wolves. Occasionally a vampire will assume the shape of a
cat or owl. But only the tiniest handful of tales, Rumanian
once more, mention even vaguely the possibility of a vampire turning himself into a bat.

Bats, of course, are nocturnal creatures associated with
dark and evil deeds, so it is not surprising that they find
their way along with cats and owls into the vampire legend.
But mention of metamorphosis into bats remained scarce,
scattered, far from being a central theme of the legend –
until the 19th century. Then European globetrotters
visited South America and brought back, along with
many other marvels, the news of the existence of a bat that
nourished itself solely and exclusively on blood. It was

promptly named after its folklorish human counterpart; and was just as promptly incorporated into vampire stories, where it has always seemed very much at home.

Finally, one of the vampire's most useful powers (again given more emphasis in fiction than in folklore), is his hypnotic ability – which enables him to send his victims to sleep, so that he may feast without a struggle. A victim will usually wake up feeling anaemic, but will remember nothing of the previous night's terrible visitor – until, of course, she (it is usually a she) notices the two small punctures on the side of her throat . . .

Perhaps it is another magical power, or perhaps just another rule of the vampire game, but the vampire seems in many tales to have the power to *recruit* his victims. Anyone on whose blood the vampire has fed – even once or twice, without causing death, say some versions – will rise up again as vampires when they finally do pass on. But this is by no means the only way that people can become vampires. The old tales stress most frequently that anyone dying in a state of sin, without the Church's blessing, risks becoming a vampire. So do exceedingly wicked men – anyone who lived rather vampiric lives before death, sometimes with the suggestion of a little dabbling in black magic. (Bram Stoker found the source of his novel in an old Wallachian history of a nobleman actually named Drakula, who misused his feudal powers and became a notorious torturer and sadist. The accounts of that man once called him a 'wampyr', the way we might call some vicious criminal a 'devil'; and Stoker took it from there.)

Balkan legends say that people return as vampires if they die after perjuring themselves, or under a curse from their parents, or as suicides, or – most prominently – if they have been excommunicated from the Church. In all these cases, the fearful shadowed immortality of the vampire operates as a punishment for evildoers. But a man can also turn into a vampire through no fault of his own. If his corpse did not receive the full funeral rites of the Church, for instance; or if, in the case of a child, he dies unbaptised (in Rumania); or if (in Greece) he had been murdered and no vengeance was exacted.

These later concepts are simply borrowings from much older ideas about why ghosts walk, to be looked at again in Chapter Three. But the vampire belief has some ideas entirely its own about how vampires happen. It has already been said that, in Rumania, werewolves were believed to become vampires after death. In Greece, anyone born on Christmas Day, or between Christmas and Epiphany, ran the risk of becoming vampires. A few tales suggest that a seventh child, if all seven are the same sex, will become a vampire – as will anyone born with a 'caul' (a portion of the amniotic membrance remaining attached to the new-born infant). These ideas are interesting reversals: in most traditions, a seventh son, or to have a caul, are signs of good fortune and special powers, of 'second sight'. In Rumania again, if a vampire gazes at a pregnant woman (a variant of the 'evil eye' idea), and if she does not have the evil erased by the Church's blessing, she will give birth to a vampire. So will a pregnant woman who does not eat salt – with its magical purifying powers. Weirdly, in some Slavonic tales, if a cat should jump over the coffin of a corpse before burial, the corpse may rise again as a vampire.

But if anyone should see the cat (sometimes a dog) performing this feat, the horror can be forestalled with a little home-made magic: putting a piece of iron in the corpse's hand, or placing hawthorn (a sacred tree, often thought to have been the provider of the crown of thorns) in the coffin. Garlic would do as well, for as everyone knows who has ever seen a horror film, vampires shun garlic. Perhaps the old superstitions imputed a special

magic to the undeniably powerful smell of garlic; certainly
it is used in the folklore of many peoples to keep off all
kinds of evil spirits, and also in many folk-medicine cures.

In the past the vampire legend briefly overlapped with
Christian demonology, so that many Christian fathers
ascribed Balkan tales of vampires to the actions of various
devils, who had entered and reanimated harmless corpses
for nefarious purposes. And while the older tales reject this
idea, insisting that the vampire is not a demon but the
original person re-inhabiting his own dead body, other
Christian elements are not entirely absent from the vampire traditions. If hawthorn and whitethorn, with their
vaguely Christian connections, are protectives against
vampires, the crucifix is even more so. The creature is evil,
whether directly Satanic or not, and therefore must shy
away from the symbol of good. So wear a cross at your
throat, the tales say, and your veins will remain untapped.
And, just to be sure, string garlic around the doors and
windows and keep a piece of silver handy, a metal univers-
ally feared by every kind of evil spirit.

If anyone suspects that a body just buried might rise
again, but if it is too late to place hawthorn or garlic in
the coffin, Slavonic legend suggests thrusting iron skewers
straight down into the earth covering the grave. The vampire will be pinned into his coffin by these sharp points. A
suicide might be buried under running water, always a
barrier to evil creatures, to prevent his return as a vampire.

If vampire activity breaks out in a locality and no one
knows which grave or tomb contains the monster, a few
traditional tests can be applied. Examine the graves for
the scattering of small holes, mentioned before, through
which the creature filters up out of his coffin. Or, Hungarian tales say, take to the cemetery a white stallion that
has never been to stud, and that has never stumbled: such
a horse will refuse to walk on the grave that houses the
vampire. In some versions of this test, the horse should be

virginal, sure-footed, but *black* – and should be ridden by an equally viriginal boy.

If none of these tests can be applied, and the vampire continues his depradations, the tradition says that the graves must be opened and the corpses examined, to find the one that has not decomposed. This activity must of course take place in the daylight, when the vampire is dormant and can do no harm. The vampiric corpse may be found not only uncorrupted, but also bearing clear signs of vampirism – red lips partly open over the fangs, blood smears on face and hands. Sometimes, in an excess of horror, the tales speak of exhumed vampires whose entire coffins and graves have been saturated and awash with blood.

Once you have caught your vampire, red-handed as it were, he can easily be finished off. For that matter, he could be finished off at night, during his activities, if anyone had the courage to look him up and shoot him with a silver bullet that had been blessed by a priest. But it was somewhat safer to disinter his body by day, and simply drive a short, sharp stake through his heart. The stake should preferably be of some sacred wood – hawthorn again, perhaps, or aspen. And some traditions say that it must be driven home with only one blow, or the magical element in the ritual would not work.

And of course there is a magical element, exactly akin to the pinning of corpses mentioned in Chapter One. Obviously any creature who has the power to turn into mist, or to filter out of a deep grave or a sealed tomb, is not going to be bothered by a bit of wood unless some powerful magic comes into play as well. Sometimes a consecrated dagger (the crucifix shape) would be used, as in Albanian traditions. Other versions insist that the vampire be decapitated as well as staked and it seems that the gravedigger's spade is usually the chosen implement for the beheading. And then a great many legends recommend destroying the vampire by the purification of fire, totally consuming coffin and contents in the flames. In one curious piece of lore, known as Bulgarian but obviously borrowed from Middle Eastern traditions, the vampire hunter can set up a special array of magic spells and so on to drive the vampire – like a *jinn* or genie – into a bottle, which is then corked and thrown onto a fire.

We will see in the next chapter that the ghostly type of revenant may walk among the living for a variety of definite purposes: revenge, unfinished tasks, messages to the living, re-enactment of some episode from the past. The vampire walks merely because he is hungry. It is motivated solely by its desire for blood – or so the more modern tales, and the vampire fictions, would seem to indicate.

But behind this blood urge, which is the most compelling and dominant element in the nature and habits of vampires, there lurks a darker truth of a sort that the 19th century could only hint at or introduce obliquely. The vampire legend is not simply as assortment of good, gory horror tales spawned by primitive superstitions about the dead. It is a blatantly *sexual* motif – riddled with eroticism, clogged with sadism and other perversions.

At one time, indeed, the sexual side of vampirism was explicit in the old Balkan tales. Vampires were said to return (rather properly) to bestow their terrible attentions on their marriage partners – though unmarried vampires visited any attractive young person of the opposite sex. And in those tales it was not just a thirst for blood that the vampire satisfied. But presumably the *mores* of the 19th century – which, like today's film censors, made it clear that murder and brutality were all right but sex was shocking – chose to leave out the explicit sex angle. All the same, enough remained in a symbolic or repressed sort of way to make the vampire myth a goldmine for Freudian psychologists.

Some of these elements can be extracted from the legend in general. The vampire bites his victims, and no one needs to have read the *Kama Sutra* or *The Perfumed Garden* to know that a bite is a kind of kiss, with sadism mixed into the eroticism. Even the vampire's appearance – the thick red lips, the hairiness (as on the palms of his hands) – corresponds to widely-held folk beliefs about what excessively sex-oriented people look like. It is not accidental, then, that male vampires tend to choose for their victims young and full-blooded girls, *vice versa* for female vampires. Here without doubt is where the incubus-succubus concept makes a direct contribution to the legend; we need pay no attention to the Victorian writers who claimed that their fictional vampires attacked ripe young girls only because the girls' blood was more nourishing.

Blood itself is not only the stuff of life but is profoundly tied up with man's sexual emotions, and has been since primeval days. So many primitives put stringent taboos on menstruating women, and some of these taboos can still be found in the superstitions of rural backwaters. Primitives and many so-called civilised peoples have also made, in the past, a fetish out of the blood-letting that should occur with a virgin bride on the wedding night. And any modern psychologist knows how often blood and blood-letting appears in the erotic fantasies of psychiatric patients. Havelock Ellis has even gone so far as to suggest that the primary motive in sex murders may be to shed blood – not necessarily to end life.

All this makes unpleasant reading, and may make some of us feel dubious about our enjoyment of fictions like *Dracula* or Sheridan Le Fanu's great 19th-century story *Carmilla* (a vampire tale, incidentally, with an undercurrent of lesbianism that would be very clear to any post-Freud reader). Even more unpleasant are the many case-histories in psychologists' files of *real* vampires. Not resurrected corpses, but living psychopaths with a special mania for the taste of blood. One such case occurred in Britain in 1949, when a man faced trial for murdering nine people and drinking their blood.

Such psychopathic types bear resemblances to certain others – those with a cannibalistic craving, those known as necrophiliacs and necrophages – who have made indirect contributions to the vampire legend (and to legends of werewolves and ghouls). The existence of such people, and such perversions – and the stories that must have spread and grown when one such person was discovered, in the superstitious past – provides a narrow but definite foundation of truth, on which all the other folklore and fictional elements could come together to create the concept of the vampire.

One further kernel of fact can be introduced, which may well have made a contribution not only to the vampire tradition, but to the whole array of legend and lore concerning walking cadavers, the living dead. The fact is that corpses have apparently been disinterred, at various times, and found to be virtually whole, uncorrupted, although they had been buried long enough for decomposition to be well under way.

Now, of course, it is likely that such accounts might not always have got their facts right, and that the exhumations may have concerned people more recently dead than the stories suggest. And these – as Montague Summers and other experts are at pains to stress – could easily have been premature burials.

Certainly in the less knowledgeable days of medicine, premature burial must have been fairly frequent, even commonplace. And if superstitious villagers found members of a community dying inexplicably (as people often did, in the 17th century, from various plagues), they might dig up a few graves and find that a recently buried corpse did not seem decomposed. If that body seemed to have changed position, and to have a fearful expression on its face and blood on its hands and finger-nails – then the villagers might well cry 'Vampire' without stopping to think that the corpse might have been buried prematurely, awakened in the grave, and died trying hopelessly to claw its way out.

But aside from the horrors of wrongful burial, there have been cases – of varying degrees of reliability – where long-dead corpses are found to be fresh and whole. Not a few Christian saints have avoided decomposition, according to religious history. As for worldly instances, there was the body of an Italian woman buried in 1820 and exhumed in 1852, found perfectly intact. One of the ex-humers accidently cut the leg of the corpse with his spade; and it was said that blood flowed abundantly from the wound (as blood always gushes when a vampire is staked in its grave), at which point decomposition began rapidly to set in.

It may be that some patches of soil, some cemetery vaults, have a chemical or other quality that inhibits de-composition. Or it may be that these tales of intact corpses are just as much folklore as the tales of the blood-greedy, living-dead vampire. But this is no place for a thorough consideration of these questions. Nor, perhaps, could many people bear to consider them too thoroughly. For them, it may be a relief to turn from the ugly background of vampire legends to the less gory, less physical (if no less horror-strewn) traditions of *disembodied* revenants.

3
Some Ghosts There Were

3
Some Ghosts There Were

PEOPLE like ghosts. If hardheaded rationalism won a total victory, and erased all the old superstitions from the minds of men, people would probably miss ghosts more than any. Collections of ghost stories crowd onto our bookshelves, newspaper editors snap up stories of haunted supermarkets or suburban bungalows, our televisions show ghosts as the leading characters not just in horror films but in domestic comedy or detective series. The disembodied spirits of the dead seem as firmly entrenched as ever in the popular imagination.

And that fact, like most facts about the popular imagination, deserves some attention. For it is not only among people who read the stories of M. R. James or who watch 'The Ghost and Mrs Muir' where the interest in ghosts is perpetuated. Civilised, intelligent people of the 1970s still seem to have experiences that they must and do classify as ghostly. And a sizable percentage of these experiences are, and always have been, the visual perception of a human or semi-human figure with aspects and attributes indicating that the figure is not an ordinary, solid, living person. This chapter will occupy itself with those aspects and attributes, in all their eerie variety.

Freud has written, regarding such experiences, that 'there is scarcely any other matter upon which our thoughts and feelings have changed so little since the very earliest times'. That may seem a somewhat obvious comment, since in early times or modern times *fear* predominates among our thoughts and feelings regarding ghosts. They are frightening because they are inexplicable, tainted with death and with the mystery of what lies beyond death. But, more directly, ghosts are frightening because they are considered to be hostile and malevolent – or, at the least, potentially so.

Some primitive peoples, among them many South American jungle tribes, believe all ghosts to be invariably hostile towards the living – as if the fact of death itself automatically imparts this hostility to the spirit. Other primitives distinguish beween those ghosts who are bound to be hostile, with good reason – such as the ghosts of enemies in battle – and others who might only *turn* hostile if provoked in some way. These latter include even the spirits of kindly ancestors: among peoples who devote some or all of their religious concerns to ancestor worship, the tribal forebears are usually seen as the guardians of the tribe's ethical and spiritual welfare. So their ghosts would be quick to punish transgressions of tribal law and taboo, and quick also to punish any slackening in the worshipful honour and praise that is their due.

Ancestor worship can be said to be one of the first, perhaps the very first, form of religious awareness that developed in man. We know now that even the cave dwellers of the Stone Age buried their dead ceremonially, and that aspects of the ceremonies (burial under or near crude altars, for instance) suggests worship of the dead. Departed forebears are central figures in many North American Indian and African religions, in the religion of the Maoris, and in some ancient Chinese and Japanese forms of worship. Japan's Shinto religion has its roots in ancestor worship, however stylised its modern forms. And the underground religion of voodoo, as mentioned in Chapter One, has more to do with peaceful ancestor worship than with orgiastic black magic.

Honouring the spirits of the fathers opens up a whole area of primitive religion that can be described as 'keeping the ghosts happy' – or making them happy again if someone has offended them. The tribesmen keep them happy with elaborate systems of offerings, rituals, and so on. If someone slips up and angers the ghosts – which anger is indicated if some disaster like disease or crop failure afflicts the tribe – then extra large offerings, special ceremonies, are brought into play, to appease or propitiate the ghosts.

But of course propitiation is just as important among societies that do not directly worship their ancestors – because of that universal fear of ghosts, whoever they were when alive. The primitive, in fact, plays safe by appeasing all ghosts. American Indian hunters would perform ritual apologies to their dead prey, especially if it was a bear or some other creature often used as a tribal totem (and so possessing supernatural powers). Elaborate sacrifices and purifications would take place after an inter-tribal war, to soothe the ghosts of dead warriors. And, of course, in a widely common cliché still in use, no one dared to 'speak ill of the dead' – not from unwillingness to dishonour a memory, but from the fear of incurring the wrath of the ghost.

Along with propitiation went the magical ways to ward off ghosts' returning. Some primitives deserted a house where a death had occurred; others set up powerful spells around the house. Primitives disguised themselves (in ritual funeral costumes) after a death so the ghost would not pester them – and folklorists see in this practice the origin of the funereal black clothing and women's veils, that is still *de rigueur* at today's funerals. Some old superstitions require that a corpse should never be taken out of a house through one of the doors, but through a special opening in the wall, later to be sealed again. The implication is that the ghost will try to re-enter as it exited, and be thwarted.

That a ghost could be so easily baulked implies a certain limitation on ghostly intelligence. So, too, does the practice of burying bodies at crossroads, especially those bodies that might produce exceptionally vengeful ghosts (hanged criminals, executed witches, and the like). Behind this idea lies the notion that the ghost will be confused by the crossroads, and be unable to find its way back to plague the living. (The motif of the cross, as a protective device against evil, seems to be incidental in this superstition – which lasted into fairly recent European history.)

Out of this general look at the universal fear of ghosts, some other folklore motifs have emerged – mainly concerning the reasons for ghosts' presence among the living. A few primitive peoples, of course, do not believe that ghosts could be anywhere else. They lack the concept of a special abode of the dead – the Elysian Fields or Valhalla or Heaven or Happy Hunting Ground. To such peoples, the spirits of the dead take up residence in nature, inhabiting trees, stones, rivers, clouds – and so exist all around the living, everywhere. But for peoples who have the idea of an afterlife going on at some mystical remove, ghosts must have some specific reasons for returning – or remaining. And the reasons that legend offers have not changed a great deal, from ancient times up to the present day.

It is clear that a great many ghosts return because they are powered by a thirst for revenge, of one sort or another. Most importantly, the ghost of a murder victim will seek out its murderer. Usually the ghost's object is mere punishment by terror, as in the ghosts that visited Macbeth's banquet table in Shakespeare's play. But just as often, and more interestingly, the ghost of the victim will return to ensure that the killer is brought to justice. In a famous

British ghost story from the 17th century, a man named William Barwick drowned his pregnant wife, then told everyone she had gone to stay with relatives. But the wife's brother saw the woman by the side of the pool where the drowning had occurred, and knew that she was a ghost. He accused Barwick of murder, and the killer confessed when the wife's body was found.

There is a comparable and more recent folktale from rural North Carolina, USA, concerning a traveller seeking a place to stay for the night. He is directed to an empty house where no one in the vicinity would dare to sleep; during the night he is visited by the ghost of a woman, the former mistress of that house, who announces that she was killed by a neighbour who remains unsuspected. She orders the traveller to accuse the neighbour; if he does not confess, she says, she will materialise at the trial and force him to. The traveller makes the accusation, and the neighbour confesses, not requiring the interruption of the trial by the ghost – who, presumably, went then to her well-earned eternal rest.

Frequently the ghost of a murder victim will appear merely to inform people that it is dead. In a story from ancient Rome, related to Cicero, the ghost of a murdered man appeared to a friend on the very night of his murder. The ghost gave extensive details about its death and the murderer's disposal of the body – so that next day the friend could not only verify that murder had been done, but could accuse the killer.

Ghosts will also grow vengeful, folklore says, towards anyone who disturbs their mortal remains. And here is a clear echo of the most deep-rooted primitive ideas about provoking ghostly wrath. For that matter, as Chapter One showed, the corpse itself might well avenge a desecration. As for ghostly retaliation, a traditional example is said to have occurred when Charles II disinterred Oliver Cromwell to symbolically hang his corpse in London's Red

Lion Square. Cromwell's ghost rose to haunt the Square in protest. In a blood-curdling old Irish tale, some rural louts who became sportive at a wake began making gruesome fun of the corpse – when four eerie men in black came and took the corpse and coffin away. One of the strangers struck the leader of the louts, whose mouth remained crooked the rest of his life, And the next day there was a new grave at the dead man's family cemetery, sixty miles away.

Ghosts will also return to terrify those who were its enemies during life – a spiteful act, but often for a justifiable vengeance. In 19th-century North Carolina, a young lady found her lover was unfaithful, and pined away – threatening before she died to come and claim the fickle man. Later, the man was returning from an evening with the other girl, when the ghost of his dead sweetheart met him and clasped his right hand, agonisingly. The hand shrivelled, and the man died within three days. Ghosts also carry on the enmities of wartime from beyond the grave: the shade of the warring Black Prince is said to reappear (in a Kent mansion) whenever enemies of England threaten the nation, and during World War Two the spirits of dead sailors were believed to haunt the coasts of Cornwall, still fighting their share of the war by luring German ships onto the rocks with falsely reassuring lights.

Those ghosts lacking a specific urge for revenge may often strike out against any living person who has the nerve to molest them. The terrible spectres that carry on the Wild Hunt (a mythical horror common throughout northern European lore though with different legendary figures at its head in different countries) prefer the living to keep out of the way. One disrespectful farmer, hearing the spectral huntsmen pass, called out to them to share their spoils – whereupon, with evil laughter, they gave him part of a human corpse. (Some versions say it was the corpse of the farmer's child.) A backwoods American story tells of a boy who saw his grandmother's ghost and tried to touch her; for this over-familiarity he was pursued and hurled into a ditch, and his side was numb for a long time where the angry old lady had grasped him.

Certain acts are said to raise ghosts, such as making unpleasant remarks about them near a cemetery; and such rude awakening can anger them. In the fens of eastern England, local lore forbids whistling on the marshes for fear of stirring the spirits; not too long ago, locals say, one man who thoughtlessly whistled to his dog was pursued to his cottage door by a fearful spectre.

But these retaliating ghosts have moved us away from the subject – why ghosts return from the beyond. A large number of stories show that many come back because of some sort of unfinished business – which can include the delivery of an important message to the living. Often the message concerns an imminent death: like the banshee that screams when Irish aristocrats are about to die, other old families have their spectral harbingers – such as the 'radiant boy' that was said to be visible in a British stately home to those who would eventually die a violent death. He was, legend says, seen by Lord Castlereagh – who years later (in 1822) committed suicide. Lord Byron's family knew of a Black Friar who appeared before the death of the current title-holder. Similarly, in the 18th century, a ghost had warned the profligate Lord Lyttelton to mend his ways, or death would overtake him – and it was proved right within days. In the 17th century the dead Duke of Buckingham vainly tried to turn his son from unpopular political acts that led to his assassination; and Josephine's shade apparently visited Napoleon some days before he died.

Occasionally, ghosts return to prevent death or disaster, and some quite modern stories exist of such protective spirits. An 18th-century American woman known as 'Ocean-born Mary', housekeeper to a pirate in New

Hampshire, still looks after the residents of her house: in 1938, during a hurricane, she was seen in the garden behind the owner of the house while trees fell all around. Neither owner or the house was touched. Also from America in the 1930s, in one instance of the famous 'Vanishing Hitchhiker' type of modern ghost (for which see later), a hitchhiking spirit in California prevented a serious collision by pulling on the handbrake – and the driver later learned that the ghost had met its death in an accident at the same spot.

Similarly, some wounded French soldiers during World War Two were helped to safety by the kindly ghost of a nun – and they later identified her from a picture as Joan of Arc. On a less dramatic or significant level, there was the ghost of a dutiful husband who returned to help his widow with her quilt-making and knitting. The wife proudly claimed he could knit half a sock in a night.

Some helpful ghosts show a surprising concern, even from beyond the grave, with materialist matters. A wealthy lady in the Isle of Skye returned after death to remind her husband to pay some neglected employees, and another lady in 19th-century Perth nobly returned as a ghost to ask a priest to pay a debt of hers, all of three shillings and tenpence. In the American South in the 1920s the ghost of a farmer visited his sons to show them where he had hidden his will.

There is an element of *reparation* in these stories of debt-paying ghosts, and other stories are more explicit about the urgings of spirit consciences. An old Welsh tale concerns a girl, seduced and deserted, who prayed that the man might have no rest in this world or the next. Naturally, after the man died, his ghost came to haunt her – but in fact begged her forgiveness and, when it was granted, never appeared again. And, also in Wales, an 18th-century preacher was approached on a lonely road by a ghost forced to walk because it had kept a silver

coin, when alive, that it should have given to the church.
The coin, it said, was hidden under a rock; the preacher
duly found it, gave it to the church, and the ghost was
never seen again.

A legion of ghost stories, still in the materialistic vein,
show revenants with a obsessive urge to reveal the hiding
places of buried treasure – as obsessive, perhaps, as man's
longlived urge to have fantasies about the finding of
treasure. Anyway, in 19th-century England, the ghost of
a miserly old lady kept appearing to people in her cottage
until someone realised that the visitations might be connected with money. The cottage was ransacked, and a
hoard of gold found in the roof. And a man in Maine,
USA, in the 1930s claimed that a ghost directed him to
some buried pirate treasure.

More usually, though, ghosts appear in tales of treasure
as the guardians, not the revealers. Captain Kidd and
other pirates were commonly said to kill a man at the site
of every treasure burying, to leave a ghostly guard. Kidd's
supposed booty is, if legend is to be believed, scattered all
along the New England coast of America; but diggings
have been interrupted by uprising ghosts on Clarke's
Island in Connecticut, Jewell's Island in Maine, and elsewhere. The tales sometimes say that treasure can be
taken up if the diggers say not a word. But of course the
ghost invariably causes someone to speak, or scream – as
in the Nova Scotian tale when four men were digging
fearfully but silently, until one of them noticed that the
number of diggers had suddenly increased to five. He
yelled, the fifth figure vanished, and the treasure magically
sank beyond recovery.

On the subject of treasure guardians, there is an interesting tale from Newfoundland, Canada, of a ghost only
too anxious to give up its treasure – because it had grown
tired of its job. Apparently one need only visit the correct
spot (on the Cape shore) at midnight and spill some sort

of blood – say, of an animal. The ghost will then be
freed, and will gratefully turn over the treasure. As yet
no one has been brave enough to try it – or no one has
found the right spot.

Like that Newfoundland ghost, many of these treasure-
revealing and task-completing spirits have come back
simply because they were unable to rest – having, as it
were, too much on their minds. So, it is said, they would
be *compelled* to walk in this world – until whatever was
bothering them was cleared up. On these lines, certainly
the most compulsively troubled ghosts of all are those
whose bodies have not received adequate burial.

From the first glimmerings of primeval history, a death
not followed by proper burial rites inevitably spawns
ghosts. The ghost might be vengeful if duly honourable
burial had been omitted purposefully; more often, the
ghost is merely miserable, and wants someone to correct
the oversight. So, in the ancient Babylonian epic, the
warrior Gilgamesh met the sad ghost of a dead and unburied friend, returned to seek his aid, in what must be
the world's oldest recorded ghost story. An exact parallel
occurs in the *Odyssey*, when Odysseus is visited by his
friend Elpenor, become a ghost because he has died accidentally and his body lies unburied.

Also from the ancient world comes a legend about the
mad Roman emperor Caligula, whose body received no
funeral honours until his ghost had made a thorough
nuisance of itself. Ireland has produced a tale about
a ghost that looked after its own funeral arrangements: a
man from Ballyferriter, buried in a graveyard in a
strange village, was conveyed by a spectral funeral pro-
cession to his family plot in his home village. Ghosts will
go to many lengths to obtain their just dues in terms
of burial: there is a rural American tale in many versions,
basically concerning some tired travellers who risk a
night in a deserted house and meet an unhappy ghost. It

leads them to a heap of human bones hidden in shrub-
bery, and promises to reveal the hiding place of a treasure
if they will give its remains proper interment. And in
Washington state, USA, in 1919, the ghost of a man who
had inexplicably disappeared returned to reveal that he
was dead by drowning, and also to guide some friends to
his corpse – which everyone had presumed lost.

Virtually all the individual ghosts mentioned so far, in
this round-up of the reasons for their return, have been
those who have stayed among the living for a limited
period of time. The vengeful ghosts complete their mis-
sion and depart; the conscience-stricken ghosts, the unburied ghosts, and so on walk until certain acts have been
accomplished, then they too disappear. Folklore implies
that such revenants are *bound* to this earth, because all
the loose ends of their lives have not been tidied up. The
revenge-seeking spirits may come back willingly, the unburied ones unwillingly; but there is an element of automatic inevitability in the returns of both types. By the
same token, the living can quickly get rid of them by
helping them to fulfil their aims: punish a murderer, pay
a debt, give proper burial to a few bones.

But other ghosts are not dismissed so readily – if at all.
These are the *recurring* type of revenant, which for our
purposes can be distinguished by the term *haunts*. In
examples already given, a few haunts have crept in, and so
the distinctions must be clarified. Haunts are generally
the ghosts said to be 'condemned to eternal restlessness'.
A very few are not condemned, but have *chosen* to remain
forever among the living – like Ocean-born Mary of New
Hampshire, mentioned earlier. But more usually the
haunting is taken to be a form of punishment for the
unhappy spirit, denied the rest and peace of the hereafter.
(It is a very simplistic view of eternal life, seeming to deny

or ignore the premise that those of the dead who deserve punishment find it in Hell or similar nether regions.)

By far the bulk of all ghosts in haunting stories are either evildoers haunting the scenes of their crimes (and this includes suicides), or the victims of evildoers haunting the scenes of their tragedies. The latter notion seems to be one of the most cruel and unjust in all folklore – but it assuredly opens the way for high melodrama in the old wives' tales.

The ancient stately homes and bleak castles (ruined or otherwise) of Europe and Britain seem to have bred as many haunts as they have mice, and most seem to be connected in popular legend to old evils and tragedies. No one needs reminding of the ghost of Anne Boleyn walking the Tower of London, whether with head under arm or not; so, too, Queen Catherine Howard's ghost shrieks in Hampton Court Palace, vainly appealing to Henry VIII for mercy as she did centuries ago. The much-married king himself seems to have slept peacefully since the day he died, which rather undermines the adage 'no rest for the wicked'.

Elsewhere, though, the wicked are very much up and about. A 17th-century English noblewoman, Lady Ferrars of Hertfordshire, much given to wild escapades such as posing as a highwayman, was said to haunt her estates until the 19th century. Also in the 17th century, an evil gentleman named Calverley killed his children and wounded his wife; he was caught and executed, and his ghost terrorised the neighbourhood of his Yorkshire mansion. Locals claimed to have seen him as late as 1874. From older times, the shade of the Emperor Nero lurked in Imperial Rome; from more recent times, an army deserter during the US Civil War was captured, then shot trying to escape – and his ghost is said still to haunt a bridge in southern Indiana where he made his escape attempt.

Suicide, of course, has always been considered a sin and a crime, and the ghosts of suicides dolefully haunt the scene of their deaths. Fillingham Castle in Lincolnshire was said to be haunted by the shade of a disappointed lover who cut his own throat; a lady who killed herself at Stanton Harcourt in the 17th century, and who was buried under a flowing pond, walks abroad when the pond dries up. (Running water, folklore tells us, is inimical to demons – in stories like this one its effect has been carried over into ghost lore.)

But rather more victims seem to haunt this world than victimisers, even aside from the vengeful kind. Here the implication seems to be that they remain in this world simply because their lives were cut off too abruptly, their deaths too unnatural. Some of the unhappy wives of Henry VIII have been mentioned; the little English princes murdered in the Tower have also reappeared, as have hosts of other kings and noblemen (Thomas à Becket among them) betrayed and killed in the long bloody history of British and European royal intrigue. On a more common level, the eternal victims also appear – like the ghost of lovely Nellie MacQuillie, a maiden of 18th-century North Carolina, killed by Indians and still haunting the brook where her death occurred.

Sometimes, when an ancestral home or a lonely highway has a constant ghost, people find it difficult to know exactly whose ghost it is – and will then attach to it, fairly arbitrarily, some macabre old tale of murder or betrayal vaguely associated with the region. But a great many haunts make very clear who they are and why they walk this earth – because their haunting is a *re-enactment* of the crimes they committed or suffered.

So a Scottish lord of Roxburghshire, said to be a black magician given to sacrificing children in his evil rites, perpetually performs those ritual sacrifices in the shadows of Hermitage Castle. So, every year on the same night, a

ghost rides up to a Lancashire castle, enters it, and on-
lookers hear the shrieks of a dying woman; then the ghost
makes his escape, as did its living original, a man who
murdered his wife in the 17th century. In that century,
too, a ghoulish Londoner looted the houses of those dead
of the Great Plague; his ghost is compelled forever to
wash spectral treasure in a rural stream, where the looter
in life had paused to cleanse his booty.

Fate magazine recently carried an account of a spectral
re-enactment seen by young British newly-weds in the
1950s. Their honeymoon cottage in Devon had been,
twenty years before, the hiding place of a runaway wife
and her lover. The newlyweds saw the shadowy figures of
the fugitives, saw also the ghost of the angry husband
enter the house, kill his wife and her lover, then throw
himself from a cliff.

It seems that when a killer must re-enact his crimes, the
ghosts of his victims by necessity must play their parts as
well. But in other cases the victims alone roam the scene
of their untimely deaths – like the abbess of an old con-
vent in York, murdered in the sweep against Catholics in
Henry VIII's time and later seen haunting a nearby
church. And in New Oreans, USA, the nude and shivering
ghost of a beautiful mulatto girl used to be seen pacing
the rooftop of a wealthy house, during one icy night each
winter. She had been the mistress of a playboy who once
jokingly suggested that she prove her love by spending the
coldest night of the year naked on his roof. She took him at
his word, tried it, and died.

In Chapter Four some instances will be noted of recurring
but invisible haunts – such as ghostly cries, footsteps, or
the noises of a re-enacted tragedy. As for the visible kind,
they seem to come in an immense variety of appearance –
as will soon be made clear – but they still have one fundamental quality in common. It was said earlier that folk-

lore seems sometimes to credit ghosts with only limited intelligence: but haunts seem to have none at all. They move, most of them, like sleepwalkers, like automatons – appearing at their set time, going through their motions, vanishing. It is as if their *image* is present without their consciousness – as if they are part of a doubly-exposed strip of film, the actions of the past superimposed on the setting of the present, replayed constantly and automatically. Most haunts, indeed, are described as wholly unaware of on-lookers, and this is especially true of the re-enacting kind. But so it is of the hundreds of others, the most common haunt of all, the ghostly figure that either stands still or walks aimlessly along a set route before disappearing.

All those hosts of grey ladies, or cowled monks in church yards, and so on fit into this category. They clog the histories of ancient buildings, and they are with us still – like the phantom of a little man in grey, seen by several employees in a London bank in 1965. Sometimes they disappear if approached, but the disappearance does not seem to be a direct reaction to the living, for they would have disappeared anyway. At other times they re-main visible even when someone has tried to touch them – without, of course, succeeding – as in the case of a tall dark clergyman who prayed regularly in a London church: one day (in 1964) the vicar of the church found himself walking right through the figure, without disturbing it.

But intermingled with the numerous tales of wandering, aimless, unaware haunts are those – fewer in number but more interesting – that do seem conscious of their surroundings. Take the East Anglian lady, murdered in her farmhouse, who perpetually walked the fields of the farm, but made herself useful now and then by frightening off apple thieves. Among the myriad grey ladies of popular legend are those often seen in the corridors and wards of Suffolk hospitals – who will sometimes bend over a patient in the most kindly comforting fashion, as if they were the spirits of long-dead but devoted nurses.

Quite a number of reputedly haunted houses are in fact haunted in only one room – where, of course, in the tales, a guest will inadvertently be placed to his extreme detriment. And of these bedroom haunters, a good few are fully aware of the living occupants – like the one which regularly visited a room in a 19th-century Bristol vicarage and shook the bed. And another British home in that century held a very aware and seemingly affectionate ghost, who distressed a spinster sleeping in the room by bestowing ghostly kisses upon her.

The USA provides a quantity of variations on one of the most interesting modern ghosts, both recurrent and aware – the Vanishing Hitchhiker. Not that it is entirely an American phenomenon: in fact it is an extremely ancient folk-tale motif, found the world over, now imposed on to the motor car and so especially prominent within the automotive restlessness of the USA. In ancient China, though, people travelled on foot – and so a Chinese tale of a vanishing hiker can supply the basic outline of the story.

A young traveller once met a lovely young girl standing weeping by the roadside. He questioned her, and she said she had lost her way. So he gallantly offered to guide her to her home. But as they approached her house, she disappeared. The young man went to the house (which the girl had described to him) and met the girl's father, who sadly said that he had had a daughter who years before had gone for a walk, got lost, and died out on the road. Her ghost appeared each year on the anniversary of her death, looking for someone to take her home.

In the mechanised version, the young girl hitches a ride, gives her home address to the driver, but mysteriously disappears just before the car reaches her house. And, usually, the mystified driver learns that such a girl once

lived at that address, but that she had died years before
in a car accident – at the spot where she had been hitchhiking.

This story has been told and re-told all over the USA,
though it seems with a slight edge to California as the
favourite locale. But there are variations. In one, the girl
is picked up at a dance, and lent an overcoat by the young
man who takes her home. As usual she disappears from
the car; the young man finds that the girl he met is in
fact dead, visits her grave, and finds his coat lying on it.
Sometimes the hitchhiker is an old woman, though pretty
young girls do understandably predominate among different versions. Sometimes the girl had met her death by
drowning, not in a motor accident – and leaves a wet
patch in the car after disappearing. Sometimes she turns
out to be a ghost with a message – usually prophetic, but
not always accurate – as in the case of the vanishing hitchhiker in Chicago, picked up just after Pearl Harbor,
who announced confidently that the war in the Pacific
would not last four months. Occasionally, the hitchhiker
does some service to the driver – like the one mentioned
earlier who pulled the handbrake and averted an accident.
Also, occasionally, the driver may make love to the girl
before she vanishes. And almost invariably – as befits the
haunting type ghost – she repeats her journey every year
on the anniversary of her death, so that the people at her
house seem fairly used to explaining the situation to un-
settled drivers.

One final variant of the hitchhiker motif has a certain
uniqueness. In 1955 a crowd of young Californians were
packed into a car driving into the San Bernardino mountains when they passed a male hitchhiker – for whom they
had no room. As they proceeded, they did not stop or
leave the road, and no other cars overtook them – yet they
saw the *same man* twice more within a few miles. The
occurrence unnerved them so much that they turned back

– and the driver apparently believed (without real reason) that by doing so they avoided some sort of accident or ill luck, of which the ubiquitous hitchhiker was a harbinger.

Certainly all of these hitchhiking haunts are fully aware of their surroundings, able to carry on conversations, and so on. Also, some can be helpful, while the others are wholly harmless and not at all frightening at the time. But another class of recurring haunts seems to be unique in its combination of awareness and a relentless malevolence towards the living. In an old Irish tale, a ghost haunted a Donegal estuary when the water was especially dangerous: it would ride as a kind of guide to anyone trying to ford the estuary – that is, leading them into danger, sometimes giving the game away by turning to glower at them with a hate-filled expression. A haunt in an Essex hunting lodge, once belonging to Queen Elizabeth I, is said to attack people at night: a fairly recent legend says that a tramp who slept one night in the lodge was found insane with terror in the morning. Many malefic haunts like luring people to suicide, among them the ghost of a Mexican workman who died during the construction of a Los Angeles bridge some years ago, and whose spirit walks the bridge trying to induce people to jump.

The foregoing survey of ghostly attributes and activities is, of course, far from comprehensive: ghost folklore contains incalculable variety, and one could go on categorising and sub-categorising for volumes. Similarly, one might spend thousands of words on listing and classifying the equally varied *descriptions* of ghosts. Some of that variety will already have emerged, in examples offered earlier, but that material and more can be gathered up here.

Primitive peoples tended to think of ghosts as dangerous, fearsome, and demonic – and their image of ghosts fitted the idea. Ghosts of ancient Japan, for instance, were said to have elongated tongues, flexible, serpentine necks, sometimes only one eye, and no legs under their flowing robes. The ghosts of ancient India had red bodies and tiger-like fangs; other primitives see ghosts as terrible giants, distorted figures of animals, and so on.

The lore of more civilised times and places has its ghostly monsters too. Most of the worst, though, come in animal form, and will be glanced at in Chapter Seven.

The more horrible human spectres tend to be less extravagantly monstrous. They might for instance be eyeless, like the famous Brown Lady of Raynham, or a grey lady of North Shields in Northumberland. A few are faceless, like a 19th-century lady ghost in Canewdon, who wore a pretty sun-bonnet over emptiness. And a very great many are headless. The ghost without a head may be a common motif because of the penchant in earlier years for execution by decapitation; at any rate, such phantoms occur in the lore of almost every nation. Sometimes, indeed, a ghost will be headless even when the person died with his head firmly attached – which indicates a folklorish urge to add extra horrific details to a good story, during transmission. So Ewen Maclaine, one-time chief of a Scots clan in Mull, haunts his family home headlessly, though he died – in battle – otherwise.

Those who remember Washington Irving's classic story will expect, rightly, that many of the headless ghosts will also be horsemen – like the one that rides a road in America's Alleghany Hills, or the knight on a white horse who haunts a road in Staffordshire. Some headless phantoms add to the goriness of the picture by carrying their heads, as Anne Boleyn is said to do, as Nellie Macquillie (mentioned earlier) does in North Carolina, as do haunts in Oxfordshire, Lincolnshire, West Sussex and scores of other places. And, for variety, heads can appear without bodies: one such, in 1953, drove a series of residents from a house in Hamburg, in spite of a cruel housing shortage.

Myriads of ghosts, as everyone knows, add to the horror of their appearance by wearing their shrouds or winding sheets. As for chain-rattling ghosts, they were probably either fettered after death to keep them from walking, or were the ghosts of chained prisoners who died in castle dungeons. Other ghosts demonstrate the method of their deaths – with bloodstains on their clothing, for instance: a victim of drowning who haunted a New Orleans bridge always appeared dripping with water and seaweed.

Then there are many ghosts who appear fairly lifelike except for some not so minor discrepancy – most commonly, a tendency to become transparent. The famous ghost of Winchcombe in Gloucestershire always seems to be an ordinary person, tall and dark, walking along a road – until the observer notices that the figure is walking two feet or so above the ground. Other lifelike spectres unnerve people by appearing to glide over the ground or floor, usually without a sound. In some cases, a lifelike ghost reveals its nature simply by wearing authentic but out-of-place period costume – as did Marie Antoinette when seen by two English ladies, in 1901, at the Trianon in Versailles, in one of the world's most famous ghost stories. And, if nothing else, a fully lifelike ghost can always prove its ghostliness by suddenly vanishing.

But with these more accurate imitations of the living, we enter upon a rather delicate area of the supernatural – containing the kind of ghosts that tend to come under the scrutiny of psychical researchers. It is a delicate area because those researchers, devoted and serious investigators into what they usually call the 'paranormal', are not interested in folklore, and dislike any attempt to relate their case histories to the weird monstrosities of the tales and legends. They do not even like the word 'ghost', preferring the slightly less loaded term 'apparition'.

Now all the ghosts in the legends mentioned so far are

apparitions, since the word means simply a visible ghost or spirit. But they are not the type of apparition that draws the attention of the Societies for Psychical Research and the like that are scattered throughout many countries. The SPRs prefer cases with an odour of authenticity about them – sane and reliable witnesses, objective, detailed, and unadorned descriptions, and so on. They sift very carefully through the cases of apparitions reported to them, and to those worthy of closer examination they bring a stringent scientific attitude, cautious, detached, and demanding. Ghosts, to the SPRs, are guilty (of being fictions) until proved factual.

Still, more than half a century of psychical research has proved none of them – not, at least, in a way that would convince ordinary people that ghosts do exist. But numerous cases in which the element of doubt is small have allowed the SPRs to set up a cluster of generalities about apparitions – and these have put paid to most of the more delicious aspects of folklore ghosts. 'True' apparitions, they say, do not leave physical traces (like footprints), nor can they be photographed – because they have no solid physical presence. Yet they seem totally lifelike on the whole, distinguishable from living persons only by the ability to disappear. They are rarely transparent, and never monstrous; their lifelike aspect is so complete that they will even cast a shadow, and will appear to open doors or pick up objects, to be aware of the presence of living onlookers.

The SPR generalities are making the point that apparitions are, in some way or another, illusory – not self-delusion, but hallucinatory. They are images imposed on our eyes, with no exterior, objective reality, And from this point come the theories, holding varying degrees of probability. The theorists note that quantities of fairly well-attested apparitions are those of the *living* – usually appearing to intimate friends or relations at some crisis-point in the life of the apparitional person. And there are also numerous and quite reliable accounts of 'point-of-death' apparitions, when some dying person appears to, again, a loved one many miles away, even though the perceiver does not know that the apparitional person is dying. Further, there are cases of the apparitions of the self – the 'wraith' or double (which folklore tends to interpret as an omen of death, so that in parts of Britain the wraith is called the 'fetch'). Examples of these sightings proliferate in many serious academic studies of the paranormal, and need not be gathered here. The point is that the SPR theorists, convinced that all these apparitions are *subjective hallucinations*, happily turn to telepathy and extra-sensory perception as a means of explaining how the hallucinations are formed. Their theories are complex, controversial, and widely different; they can be safely bypassed here in their details, though not without noting some problematic questions that they do not satisfactorily answer.

First, if ESP is *not* brought in to explain the perception of hallucinatory apparitions, there is little else that can do that job – other than the views of rationalist sceptics (who will say that people who see apparitions were dreaming, deranged, or deluded). Yet if ESP *is* brought in, the process becomes the pursuit of the inexplicable by the unfathomable – for not even the SPRs can say what telepathy is, nor prove to everyone's satisfaction that there even *is* such a thing.

Secondly, even if we accept that ESP exists and that 'phantasms of the living' are some form of visual mind-to-mind communication, what of the many cases, as authentic as possible, of apparitions of the dead? Would they not lead to a clear assumption that the conscious mind can survive death?

Now of course millions of people do make that assumption – among them, the purveyors of 'spirit messages' within the spiritualist movement. But the SPR, seeking as it does some scientific basis for its conclusions, cannot take the hereafter on faith. And yet it must realise that man is no closer to *proving* survival after death than he was in the ghost-ridden ancient world. So, whatever the SPR antipathy for the horrors of the old wives' tales, the door stays open for a lot of old-time spooks and phantoms to go on haunting – and delighting – the modern world.

Yet, perhaps, not as many as once there were. Modern psychical investigations, with up-to-date equipment and realist attitudes, have tended to undermine some fine old traditions and legends. By way of illustration and conclusion, take the most famous case of all – the story of Borley Rectory.

Borley was a decrepit old pile in Suffolk with more than its share of 19th-century ghosts – a spectral nun, a coach and horses, a girl in white, a deceased rector, and more. In 1929 these tales came to the ears of a journalist and self-appointed ghost hunter named Harry Price, who began an investigation that went on for years. Price lived in the place briefly, sent in teams of assistants, wrote two books about it. Borley (and he) gained immense fame – but it did not last past Price's death in 1948. Some years later, three dedicated and professional psychical researchers wrote a damning book about Price and Borley, scoffing at the meagre evidence of ghostly activity, and casting doubt on some of that evidence in a way that implied that Price, or others, had faked it.

Without going into details, the story can be taken as the most serious controversy in modern British psychical research. But one of the most curious points about it all is the total alteration in the nature of Borley's haunts, as soon as Price appeared on the scene. Where there had been good old-fashioned nuns and coaches and other apparitions, there were apparitions no longer. Instead, almost as Price crossed the threshold, the apparitions vanished forever – and the *poltergeists* took over. Stones and other objects flew about, weird noises were heard, 'ghostly' writing appeared on walls.

The change seems rather a sad comedown. The old-style ghostly figures at least had some dignity and grandeur about them. Poltergeists, as the next chapter will show, are generally just destructive and rather childish nuisances. They are also, it must be added, the form of haunting that is most easily and undetectaby faked. But whether this is a contributory cause or not, the fact remains that the splendid old apparitional ghosts and haunts, who used to freeze people's blood from time immemorial, are dwindling away under the no-holds-barred scrutiny of today's investigators – and the scoffing of today's scientific rationalism. Only the poltergeist continues unabated, on his merry, messy, mystifying way.

4
Invisible Vandals

4

Invisible Vandals

THE poltergeist receives its name from the adoption into English of a German compound meaning 'noisy ghost' (or, as some writers more attractively translate it, 'racketing ghost'). But though screams, footsteps, knockings, and general 'bumps in the night' are central to its repertoire, the poltergeist does not merely make noises. Unlike the average visible ghost or apparition, the poltergeist can have a definite physical effect on the environment. It can move things, throw things, wreck things. And it has been doing so for centuries, without any noticeable let-up in modern times.

Stones always seemed to rank among its favourite weapons: inexplicable showers of stones have been among the marvels of many past ages. In 1821 stones fell sporadically on a house in Cornwall for all of five days, though the occupants took every precaution to ensure that the attack was not from practical jokers or other human hands. No such question arose with a stone-throwing poltergeist in Belgium, in 1913: it hurled its missiles through windows, terrifying eye-witnesses because the stones did not shatter the glass but *perforated* it with neat holes – sometimes making spiral patterns of holes in the glass.

But the poltergeist's invisible hand can throw just about anything – sometimes highly unexpected things, but more often handy objects like kitchen utensils, pots and pans,

books and bricks and vases, and so on. Dishes flew around
a poltergeist-invaded caravan parked at Leigh in 1963;
the previous year, in a Berkshire supermarket, an invisible thrower flung groceries and jars of sweets round the
shop, though it seemed above all to prefer moving packets
of bicarbonate of soda from one place to another. In 1927,
in Czechoslovakia, a poltergeist switched from throwing
stones to throwing money – coins or notes. In Durweston,
Dorset, in 1895, a lady was pelted by stones, boots, beads,
shells, thimbles, a pencil, and – not unpleasantly – flowers.

If the last-mentioned poltergeist seemed to be rather
delicate in the wrist, preferring lighter objects, others
have brought more strength to their activities. Scores of
cases relate the flight of great rocks, heavy chairs, desks,
and equally cumbrous objects. Yet, oddly enough, as
several authorities have noted, few cases of serious or
permanent injury result from these apparently demonic
barrages. In a famous Austrian case of 1818, large stones
and other dangerous objects flew through the air as thick
as hail, but seemed to have their own radar systems. The
objects would veer away from people, or would suddenly
slow, if a collision with a person was unavoidable, so as
only to touch them lightly. At one point a huge wooden
bucket dropped (from the ceiling, it seemed, though no
one saw it rise) straight down on to a group of observers –
but touched none of them, though missing only by inches.
The Austrian poltergeist may have been a vandal and a
troublemaker, but it was clearly no killer.

Many accounts of poltergeists who throw things have
noted the curious movement of the missiles – above all,
that they can swerve and curve in the air, accelerate or
decelerate, occasionally even hover. Of course, some of
the cases that will be mentioned involved a more furious
hurling of sizeable objects, especially those that would
smash satisfyingly against a wall or floor. But there are
equal numbers of cases where the objects travelled almost

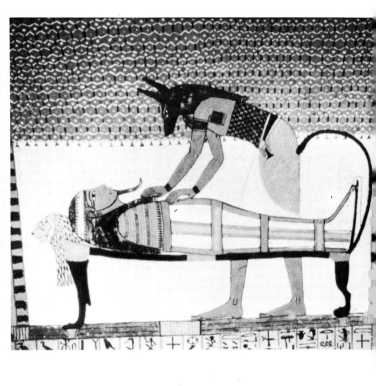

1. This frieze, from the tomb of Sennedjen, shows Anubis, the Egyptian god of the dead and inventor of embalming.

2. Mummy of a cat from Abydos Roman Period after 30 BC.

3. Vampyre Bat, from an engraving of 1800.

4. *Above*. Christopher Lee as Dracula, Prince of Darkness.

5. *Opposite above*. Dining-room at Borley Rectory, the 'most haunted house in England', the scene of violent poltergeist phenomena in the 1930s: legends of a murdered nun and visions of headless men and a ghostly coach and horses were also associated with it.

6. *Opposite below*. Alleged spirit messages on the wall of Borley Rectory before a fire gutted it. The writing was later believed to have been that of Mrs Marianne Foyster, wife of the tenant, to whom the messages were addressed.

Marianne

~~[scribble]~~

I CANNOT UNDERSTAND
TELL ME MORE

Marianne,

~~[scribble]~~

I STILL CANNOT UNDERSTAND
PLEASE TELL ME MORE.

7. A masterpiece by one of the most famous of spirit photographers, William Hope, who gave thousands of sittings in the early 1900s. His technique was double exposure – the sitter's plate being replaced by a prepared plate with an 'extra' dressed in 'ectoplasmic' cheese cloth already on it.

8. Albert Lucas claimed he could see the spirits of dead people when in trance, and as he was a competent portrait painter, his paintings and sketches of spirits seen often bore an uncanny resemblance to what they actually looked like during life. The painting is of a figure allegedly seen in trance by Mr Lucas of Dorset, in the 1950s.

Waarhafftige Begebenheit!
Mit einem verbannten Wolff: welcher im 1685ten Jahr im
Margrafthim Onolzbach etliche Kinder weggetragen und ge-
fressen, letzlich den 9 Octobris in einem Brunen Zu Neises bij Eschenbach gefangen und ertödet, so dann dieser figin nach, aufgehangen Worden.

Ich Wolff ein Grausams Thier, Ein Fresser vieler Kinder.
ich achtet sie viel mehr, als fette Schaaf und Rinder.
Ein Han der bracht michtumb, Ein Brünen war mein Todt,
nun henck an Galgen ich, zu aller Leuthe spott;

bij Georg Jacob Schneider fec
Rothenburg auf finden

9. *Above.* A spectral carriage.

10. *Below.* The werewolf of Eschenbach which carried
children off and ate them and was drowned in 1685. A
'true story' from the Nuremberg MS.

as if they were being carried – by invisible hands – at
walking pace. The lady of Durweston, mentioned above,
noted that some of the objects thrown at her came *round*
the door, and at such a slow speed that, if thrown by a
human agency, they would never have reached her. Some
missed her, and fell to the floor on a straight slanting line,
not a curved ballistic-type trajectory. Other witnesses to
similar attacks comment that the missiles often seem to
come straight down, out of nowhere – or to *materialise* in
mid-air, and then begin their flight. (These objects – the
ones that appear from nowhere, as opposed to those
already in the place before they are thrown – have been
termed 'apports' by the psychical researchers. We will meet
the term again in Chapter Five). And, fairly often, the
objects thrown will be found to have become curiously hot
– often too hot to handle. This oddity remained true of
objects, in some cases, that were thrown from the outdoors
during very cold weather – as in an Icelandic visitation,
to be looked at again later.

But a goodly number of poltergeists, like people, generally prefer to save their strength. They will *push* heavy
objects around – mostly large articles of furniture – rather
than throwing them. In a Cheshire case in 1952 a heavy
dresser was seen moving across the floor; in an Irish case
in 1910 a bed was lifted slightly in the air; and in Berkeley,
California, in the 1940s, beds with sleepers in them moved
across the floor. A West Virginia story concerns a deserted
house still containing all the furniture, because the owner
apparently wanted it that way: if anyone disturbed the
arrangement of the furniture, odd noises would soon be
heard from within the house, and next day the articles
would all be back in their original positions.

Two other unseen ghosts, though not furniture movers,
had a similar liking for keeping things as they originally
were. But in their cases, as related by Christina Hole, the
sites they tended were the spots where they met violent

deaths. A Lancashire man was robbed and murdered in 1824, so brutally that his crushed head made a deep imprint in the soft ground. That imprint, in spite of the likelihood of its silting up after rain, is said to have remained visible for decades. Various investigators apparently tried placing stones or earth in the hole, and one man filled it completely and sodded it over. But on the following day the intruding objects would be found flung to the side, and the depression as clear as ever. And in 18th-century London a duel fought by two brothers over a woman led to the legend of the Field of Forty Footsteps – for the footprints of the duellists (who both died on the field) remained clear on the ground, and no grass would grow on them.

But back to the movement of objects by poltergeists. Some of the gentler ones have shown a liking merely for opening and closing doors, like the one that oppressed the family of Samuel Wesley (father of the famous evangelist) in 1716, constantly lifting latches and flinging doors open even when members of the family tried to hold them shut. In Oxford early in this century an invisible ghost that haunted a particular room in its house would invariably open and shut a door of the room, then open and shut a door on the opposite side – as if something had simply passed through the room on the way elsewhere. There were no phenomena anywhere else in the house.

In 1964 a typical throwing ghost added a new variation, in its tormenting of a house in Calais, France. It drew crosses on the ceiling with a tube of toothpaste. Less obstreperous are the unseen spirits with a penchant for running machinery: a sewing machine running by itself in California in 1944, farm machinery starting up on an Ontario farm earlier in this century. These mechanically-minded poltergeists have something in common with the peaceful and likeable ghost of an Oxford vicar, who persisted after death in removing books from the library shelves in the vicarage and especially winding up his collection of antique clocks. But he ceased these harmless activities when the new vicar, pointedly but rather unkindly, removed the clocks elsewhere.

By way of contrast, there are the many far-from-likeable poltergeists: not content with making things fly through the air, or furniture slide along the floor, they go all out for destruction, with that apparent delight in pointless smashing and wrecking that marks the true vandal. In a case of destructive desecration, a number of coffins were tumbled around inside a sealed vault in 19th-century Barbados. The likelihood of a human or natural agency in this case was slim – for the vault was hewn out of solid rock, no earth tremors had been noted in the area, and the coffins were made of lead, each requiring six or eight men to lift it.

It also seems that – as with the present-day relationship between vandalism and newspaper editors – the more malicious an attack is, the more publicity it receives. For instance, one of the 19th-century's most notorious 'hauntings', in Shrewsbury in the 1880s, involved not only the frenzied flight of kitchenware but explosive fires throughout the house – fires that were at first illusory, but not later. While every portable object in the house flew dangerously through the air (including a heavy sewing machine, smashed against a wall) the clothing of two children of the household burst into flames – real flame, it seems.

But at least everyone more or less kept their heads, though the sensation brought sightseers from miles around. The same kind of attention was paid to the so-called 'Amherst Mystery', one of the more famous of poltergeist cases and another one of the nastiest.

The events began tentatively, in the house of the Teed family in Amherst, Nova Scotia, in 1878. Mrs Teed's young sister, Esther Cox, seemed to be the focus of the manifestations: she complained of a scratching under her bed, then of feeling strangely ill. Soon the build-up began. The household was terrified by loud, explosive noises without apparent cause; Esther's bedclothes were being weirdly disturbed (in full view, it seems, of witnesses), and her body at times swelled up fearfully as if being inflated like a balloon. Soon household objects began flying round the rooms; and then the poltergeist sent a direct message of its malevolence – by writing on the wall: 'Esther Cox, you are mine to kill'.

By the time the journalists and sensationalists arrived hungrily on the scene, the mystery (in the words of Sachaverell Sitwell) degenerated into farce. Lighted matches began falling from the ceiling, and Esther – who was occasionally found stuck with pins like a pincushion – heard a disembodied voice threaten to burn the house down. Several times the poltergeist tried to do so, but was thwarted by quick action and pails of water.

Both the house and Esther survived the attacks – and later commentators have wryly noted that when she was seriously and legitimately ill (with diphtheria) at one point during the 'haunting', not one tiny manifestation occurred. Nevertheless, most commentators give her the benefit of the doubt: if she was involved in any conscious fraud and trickery, it was only in the later stages of the phenomena, when she had been delighted by the public sensation the early stages had caused. As for *unconscious* trickery, that is another question.

As every sensible writer on the poltergeist phenomenon has made clear, the destructive, throwing type creates the kind of havoc and damage that resembles the kind of violence which might come from an irresponsible, malicious, and probably mentally disturbed child. And, these writers quickly add, in a high percentage of cases such phenomena take place in houses where there is, indeed, such a child or adolescent – in some way disturbed, or psychologically maladjusted, or simply suffering the malaise of puberty.

Many of the cases mentioned so far have had a child or adolescent on the scene, like nineteen-year-old Esther Cox in Amherst, or a thirteen-year-old girl in Shrewsbury. In more recent times, there have been some striking American cases: one at Seaford, Long Island, in 1958, investigated by police and by Duke University parapsychologists, affected a family with two pubescent children, though both were absolved in any involvement with trickery. In 1957, in Hartville, Missouri, a destructive 'throwing' poltergeist invaded the home of the Ward family, who had a nine-year-old daughter named Betty. That case was investigated by Mr W. E. Cox, also of the Duke University Parapsychology Laboratory – and though he felt that Betty was faking a good many of the phenomena, it was as if she was *helping* the poltergeist, not creating it. For Mr Cox himself, an unassailable witness, saw a few of the phenomena occur before his very own eyes, with no possibility that Betty or anyone else could have caused them.

But it is a long step from the correlation of disturbed children with poltergeists to an explanation of how the children do it – if they do. Most people, of course, prefer not to consider any alternatives to the idea that all poltergeist cases have been either delusions or frauds. Even Frank Podmore, a leading British psychical researcher, dismissed the phenomena as nothing 'which could not have been done by a girl or boy of slightly more than average cunning and naughtiness'. And of course trickery *has* been the root of many cases, especially the famous 'Cock Lane' ghost that had Dr Johnson's London buzzing. Still, all those earnest eyewitness accounts, rather like Mr Cox's in Hartville, tend to add up. And therefore people must ask: if poltergeists are not delusions or fakes, what are they?

For one thing, as was hinted before, they might be unconscious fakes – the child, say, or some other person, pro-

ducing the phenomena while sleepwalking or in some sort
of hysteric trance state. 'Hysteric', of course, is a blanket
word glibly covering a multitude of half-understood
mental disorders, but it gives a general picture of the state
of mind involved. And people in such a state have, in
the psychologists' casebooks, evinced unnatural strength,
which might account for the objection that adolescent
children are not physically capable of hurling heavy
objects, furniture and the like, through the air.

But then what of all those heaps of evidence, not to be
dismissed too readily, concerning phenomena that the
children at the scene could not possibly have caused? Mr
Cox saw a heavy lantern overturn on a chair where it had
been solidly placed, and he was the closest person to it.
And what of all those objects sailing with majestic and
eerie slowness through the air, or changing direction in
mid-air? All of them delusion, every one? Or fraud, or lie?

Perhaps, yes. But the parapsychologists, giving their
benefit of the doubt, bring out a theory that seems to be
straight out of science fiction. Psychokinesis (PK): the
ability to move objects by exerting some kind of mental
force on them, sometimes called 'telekinesis'. When Dr
J. B. Rhine was carrying out his famous experiments at
Duke University, he and those who followed him gathered
vast quantities of statistical evidence about dice throwing,
and claimed that it was difficult to explain the results
without accepting the idea of some form of PK. Now this
is no place for the pros and cons of the wild controversy
that has ranged around Rhine since the 1930s. But two
points must not escape us. First, even if we accept the idea
of PK (and it is unquestionably far from being proved to
most scientists' satisfaction), there is considerable differ-
ence between mentally affecting the roll of two small dice
and mentally causing chairs or buckets or heavy stones to
hurtle through the air with fine directional control. And
secondly, with the involvement of PK we have the same

problem that we had with the ESP theories about apparitions. We know virtually nothing about PK except the label we arbitrarily give it – not even, for certain, if there is such a thing. And so, again, it is the pursuit of the inexplicable by the unfathomable.

The stone-throwers, furniture movers, and house wreckers may be the most familiar (because most publicised) kinds of poltergeists, but they do not exhaust the list of poltergeist types – included in which is just about every kind of unseen ghost or invisible haunting. After all, we have four other senses besides vision; and although hardly anyone has recorded the event of *tasting* a ghost, folklore and psychical research have thrown up many instances in which ghostly phenomena have been manifest in terms of touch and hearing and even smell.

Even apparitions can have their tactile effects: one of the most common sensations associated with a visible spectre is the feeling of unnatural chill that accompanies the vision. But sometimes the weird cold emerges by itself, presumably accompanying an unseen haunt. During a clairvoyant's reconnaissance of some of Britain's most haunted stately homes (in 1961), a lady writer accompanying him noticed an instance of this eerie chilliness at Longleat, home of the Marquess of Bath. Referring to a traditionally haunted passage in the mansion, she described the sensation as 'a dead, flat cold with sharply defined boundaries, so that if you moved back a few paces you were out of it'. And during the late 19th century in America's Alleghany Mountains, a lady was certain that her dead sister was haunting the house because of the similar inexplicable icy coldness of certain spots in the house.

But usually the tactile ghosts make themselves felt in a more definitely human way. Sometimes, however invisible they are, their 'bodies' have enough substance to leave imprints behind. Thus Welsh legend tells us of a haunted

bedroom in a house near Aberystwyth, where the bed holds
the marks of a human form lying on it – however often the
bed is smoothed, or re-made. In recent years a story came
out of Sheffield of a latch-lifting and door-opening poltergeist who also tended to take little rests on a comfortable
sofa – when the imprint on the cushions, of someone
sitting, was clearly apparent. In 1957, in the island of
Jersey, a lady's house was so troubled with poltergeist
noises that she retired to bed to rest her nerves. But no
rest was to be had – for something came into her room
and, unseen but definitely felt, lay down beside her. And
in 1956 a seventy-one-year-old widow (again in Sheffield)
asked for a new council flat because a similar something
insisted on sharing her bed, making the mattress sink and
the springs creak.

Occasionally the touchable poltergeist uses its physical
power to be of some use, as when an unseen hand clutched
a miner in Montana, in the 1920s, and snatched him from
a tunnel just before a cave-in. Or when a similar unseen
hand, in 1943, took over the wheel of a British ship off the
China coast during a fog. The helmsman and officers
fought its hold on the wheel, but unavailingly: its strength
slowly forced the ship out to sea, away from the shoreline.
Then, still wrestling with the wheel, the third officer
looked up with horror to see a cluster of submerged rocks
sliding past the ship on the coast side – rocks which the
vessel would assuredly have struck, had not the unknown
taken a hand in the steering.

But we have by now heard enough about poltergeists to
know that such kindliness is the exception. The rule is
malicious trouble-making, and is as true of the tactile
ghost as of the stone thrower. Sometimes, indeed, the tactile kind becomes a thrower in his own right – as in an
Icelandic case in 1907, investigated by psychical researchers, in which a man was forcibly thrown out of bed,
tossed into the air, and so on. Other poltergeists have also

preferred to throw people rather than objects, like the 18th-century haunt of Calverley Hall in Yorkshire, who flung a clergyman out of his bed three times in one night.

Then some of the touchable spirits make injurious attacks on individuals (again breaking that general rule about personal harm to observers, along the lines of the unpleasant Amherst case). A 19th-century ghost in a Welsh farmhouse tired of throwing things and began hitting people – though once or twice it disarmed everyone by stroking or patting. Another aggressive visitant, in 19th-century Devon, regularly and cruelly beat the servants in the haunted house, and several witnesses attested to the marks and contusions left by its unseen fists. The famous Drummer of Tedworth, whom we will meet again later, sometimes put its drumsticks down and slapped people; the equally famous Bell 'witch', who will also reappear in this chapter, frequently pummelled poor Mr Bell; and the poltergeist that infested the home of the Wesleys in the 18th century several times pushed Samuel Wesley around in a rough manner. In more recent times, a German poltergeist familiarly called 'Gus the Nazi', who upset a Bavarian town in 1949, paid special attention to German girls who 'fraternised' with soldiers of the occupation army – striking them, throwing things at them. In at least one case he cropped a girl's hair (as people had done during the war to girls who associated with German occupation forces) with unseen scissors, but in full view of the girl's mother.

But no case of personal attack by poltergeist has been more of a cause célèbre than that of a thirteen-year-old Rumanian girl in the 1920s, plagued by a haunt that was given to biting. The story attracted so much attention that the girl, named Eleanore, was brought to Britain to be studied by leading psychical researchers. In front of their eyes, the wounds consistently appeared: scratches, gouges, weals – whatever they were called they looked like tooth-marks – and they appeared on Eleanore's flesh without visible cause.

This case has reminded many experts of all the cases of 'stigmata' – including marks on the flesh imitative of the wounds of Jesus – that have occurred in the annals of religious history. Many psychologists will agree to the weirdness of physical phenomena accompanying that con-dition labelled 'hysteria'. Hysterics, people under hypno-sis, and people with psychosomatic illness seem to exert a strange mental control over their bodies: the creation of causeless bite-marks might not be beyond this power. And it is equally interesting that the girl Eleanore gave a name to the 'ghost' that bit her: *Dracu*, Rumanian for 'devil' or 'evil spirit', strangely reminiscent of the name of another biting monster whom we met in Chapter Two.

Ghosts manifesting themselves to the sense of *smell* tend to be rarities, but folklore contains enough to make them worthy of mention. Of course some bloodcurdling old legends have been dressed up with extra horrors, by genera-tions of old wives making a good story even better, and some of these additions include nasty or demonic smells. So the mysterious Drummer of Tedworth was accompanied by a smell of sulphur, lending a nice hellish touch to the tale – and British folklore contains one or two animal ghosts with this sulphurous odour of the pit about them. A fairly recent tale from Truro, Cornwall, concerns a house 'haunted' by a pervasive but unexplained smell of lavender – unexplained until the tenants heard that the deceased lady owner of the house always carried a lavender bag. In 17th-century America, a situation of thwarted love and murder ended in a burning alive of a young girl – who is said still to haunt the scene of her death with a pungent smell of smoke. And in 1965, a man in Kent complained of a ghost in his house that apparently liked a few drinks –

because its haunting occurred in the form of an over-powering but causeless smell of whisky.

The purveyors of ghost legends usually make the assumption that poltergeists, for all their invisibility, are human ghosts – that is, the shades of dead people, who for some unknown reason remain unseen. It is an assumption that must be taken, if at all, on faith – except when the unseen spirits make their humanity explicitly clear. Many weird tales concern haunted houses in which the manifestations are simply the sound of human footsteps where no feet are – as with a light-footed Suffolk ghost in the 19th century. She also went about accompanied by the sound of a silk dress rustling, to convince listeners of her femininity, and ghost lore is full of similar cases of this rustling sound. It appeared in a Somerset house in 1946, for instance, along with the usual footsteps, but with the distressing addition of the sound of feminine sobbing.

Perhaps that weeping ghost was eternally reliving the aftermath of some tragedy, in an audible parallel to the visible haunts, discussed in Chapter Two, who *re-enact* their deaths, or their crimes, or other crises. Such recurring re-enactments staged for the ear alone include the groans that used to chill the blood of guards at the Tower of London – said to be the ghost of Guy Fawkes recalling his torture on the rack. And Wayland Wood in Norfolk was said to be haunted by the despairing cries of long-dead children who were abandoned there – the origin of the 'Babes in the Wood' story.

In Scotland centuries ago, during an inter-clan feud, a group of men were locked in a remote castle room and left to starve to death – and legend says that their ghosts still cry for food from behind the door of that room. And in Hampshire in the 1820s a servant killed his master by walling him up alive, beneath the house, where his ghost perpetually beats against the bricks as the dying man had done.

In New Hampshire, USA, there is a body of water called Haunted Lake because of the groans and screams heard there – the scene of a 19th-century murder. And some New England sea-coast marauders, who drowned in a storm one night in the late 18th century, still shriek for help from the water, as does the unseen ghost of a lady drowned by pirates off the New Hampshire coast.

In more modern times, British tourists visiting Dieppe, France, in 1951, clearly heard a re-enactment of that desperate battle of World War Two. And the British writer, D. C. Horton, once related (on BBC radio) a re-enactment he had heard in Calcutta – the noise of carriage wheels, a shot, and a scream. He later learned that these noises could always be heard at that spot on the same night each year – recalling a scene of thirty years before when a jealous lover, pursuing the carriage containing his girl and successful rival, fired a shot that killed the girl.

On a less depressing note, many unseen haunts bring a little ghostly music into the lives of the living – like the tempestuous lady of New York state who (when alive) liked to awaken her house guests with organ music at dawn, and still sometimes rouses the household that way although she has been dead since 1870. Or the friendly British publican who, in 1965, frequently blew a trumpet in his Buckinghamshire pub to tell drinkers when time was up. He did so when he was alive, and he was still doing so months after he died.

Also in modern times, people in Anglesey have heard the voice of a dead opera singer near where the singer's house once stood; and the ghostly chanting of monks has been heard emanating from the ruins of an abbey near Beaulieu, one of Britain's stateliest homes. Bell ringing in theoretically deserted churches has spawned poltergeist tales, though as often as not some human prankster could easily have been at the ropes. Less readily dismissed was the unexplained sound of bells ringing in a Suffolk house for fifty-three days, in the 1840s. In 19th-century Boston, servants' bells rang when no living hands pulled them – and even when they had been wholly disconnected. A Rhode Island poltergeist in the 1880s rang a factory bell, for months after a night watchman had hanged himself from the bell rope. When the bell was removed, the haunt turned his attention to running the factory machinery.

The Drummer of Tedworth, alluded to earlier, must be classed among musical poltergeists, though his music seldom pleased his audience. In the 17th century a Wiltshire magistrate imprisoned a drummer for begging and confiscated the drum. It seemed as if the beggar, from prison, sent his drum music to the magistrate's house to wreak vengeful havoc. Not only did the phantom drum beat all night long, but other horrors happened besides – physical attacks on members of the household, a pervading stench of sulphur, and a few flying objects. The drummer was promptly charged with witchcraft, but was acquitted. The infestation ended, however, only when the drummer was successfully prosecuted for stealing a pig, and sentenced to transportation.

As old houses settle over the years, the creaks and bumps from their woodwork may have given rise to many minor legends of audible poltergeists – but some such cases, generally termed 'knocking' or 'rapping' poltergeists, seem too elaborate to be so easily explained. Like the thumping noises in a small village in Wales, which came (at night) from the shop of a man who was both carpenter and undertaker – and which always presaged a death in the village. In West Virginia earlier in this century, a woman was constantly annoyed by knocks at her door, though no one was ever there when she answered. Suspecting mischievous children, she kept watch on the door – and heard the knocks while watching, though no one had appeared.

Sometimes a knocking poltergeist will communicate in a rough-and-ready code – as did the object-throwing ghost of Durweston, mentioned before, who answered questions with so many knocks for yes and so many for no. A legendary hero of West England, called Wild Edric, is said to sleep beneath some Shropshire hills (when he is not leading the 'Wild Hunt' alluded to in Chapter Three); he directs lead miners to the best lodes by knocking on the cavern walls. And a Belgian knocker chatted extensively with the people of its house by a code of rapping on the wall. But of course the best-known instance of a rapping and communicating ghost happened to a family in New York state in the last century and, unwittingly, gave birth to an occult movement that has now – as the next chapter will show – reached the status of a full-scale religion.

Some invisible ghosts do not find it necessary to work out rapping codes, for they have voices and use them readily. Often the voice merely screams – like the weird cry from an empty field near a house in Sussex, in 1964. The chilling sound lasted fifteen minutes – and the man who heard it later learned that on the same night his father had died, miles away. That man instantly thought of the Irish legend of the banshee, the spirit that shrieks when the head of certain families passes on. Fairly recently several students in Dublin claimed they heard a banshee scream, and that next morning one of them received the news of his mother's death that night.

A well-known folklorist named Thomas Westropp in 1910 wrote an account, attested to by witnesses whose reliability he certified, of a wildly haunted house in County Clare – full of footsteps and door slamming, but also of eerie whispers, sobbing, muttering, shrieks, and wild laughter. The so-called 'Bell Witch' seems to have been an equally demonic poltergeist, in its relentless haunting of John Bell, a 19th-century Tennessee farmer. (The word 'poltergeist' had not then been adopted into the language;

'witch', then as now, was a handy label.) The symptoms began mildly – with strange scratching noises, snatching of bedclothes, and the like. But soon Bell was suffering torments – not the least of which was the spirit's announcement, in a clear feminine voice, that she intended to make Bell suffer and eventually kill him. But she failed to say why.

Various inexplicable pains and swellings began to afflict Bell, with no physical causes – especially a swelling of the tongue that virtually prevented him from eating or drinking. As he grew weaker (from terror and exhaustion as much as from lack of sustenance), other members of the family suffered mild ailments – all but twelve-year-old Betty, whom the 'witch' liked. In fact, the spirit once provided Betty with a spectacular 'apport' birthday present: a basket of fruit, appearing from nowhere, which the witch's voice claimed had come – just then – from the West Indies. (Elaborations of the story later said that 'experts' had found the basket itself to be of legitimate West Indian weave.)

In the end, his house echoing with the screeching laughter and derisive comments of the murderous poltergeist, John Bell duly lay down and died. Controversy still rages – over how much of the story is exaggeration, how much fraud, how much, if any, reliable.

Other talking poltergeists may have seemed more pleasant company – like the 19th-century Welsh stone-thrower, mentioned before as a ghost that struck people, which varied its activities with reasonable conversation and even violin playing. Or a somewhat chummy voice from Saragossa, Spain, in 1934, which issued from a kitchen chimney place and loved a nice chat with members of the household. Another friendly talker addressed many interested clergymen (in 14th-century Provence) on the subject of his experiences in the life hereafter: it claimed, for instance, to be undergoing its passage through purgatory at that time. And a rather schizophrenic talking ghost in Quebec, Canada, in the 1890s, alternated between periods of foul language (and throwing things) to periods of great contrition when it promised not to do it again.

Dr Nandor Fodor, the American psychologist and expert on the occult, has suggested something like 'unconscious ventriloquism' to explain these cases of disembodied voices. It may be a theory somewhat easier to swallow than the 'psychokinesis' (unconscious or not) brought in to account for the poltergeists who throw objects or move furniture. But in any case, the poltergeist seems to be a sufficiently permanent and universal phenomenon to warrant some close and serious attention – to see, for instance, whether anything at all is left once the conscious, wilful faking and the unconscious, hysteric, or psychosomatic trickery have been weeded out.

5
The Cult of the Poltergeist

5

The Cult of the Poltergeist

APPROPRIATELY enough, it all began in Arcadia. Not the never-never land described in the Elizabethan fantasy by Sir Philip Sidney, but the township of that name in New York state, where in the 1840s a family named Fox lived in a village called Hydesville. Their house had a small but firm reputation for being haunted; and, thus pre-programmed, as it were, the Fox family found their share of haunts – the poltergeist kind, various knocks, thumps, raps, rumblings of unseen furniture being moved. The two daughters of the family – Margaret, aged fifteen, and Kate, twelve – were frightened at first, but seemingly became familiarised with the noises. They even bestowed a pet name on their 'ghost', calling him 'Mr Splitfoot', a reference to the devil's cloven hoof.

Then one Friday night in 1848 the girls fell by accident into communication with their rapping poltergeist. They had been echoing its knocks by snapping their fingers: young Kate then said 'Mr Splitfoot, do as I do', and snapped her fingers (or clapped her hands – versions vary) a specific number of times. An equal number of ghostly knocks replied.

Soon the family had evolved a simple code – a given number of raps for letters of the alphabet, and for yes or no – and were deep in conversation with their poltergeist. It readily informed them that it was, indeed, a spirit, that it intended them no harm, that in life it had been murdered in the house. Needless to say, in a day or two people had gathered from all around the locality to follow the story as the conversations continued. In their hearing, the manifestation directed the Foxes to dig under the house for human remains: of course they found some, or thought they did, although we have only the word of the Foxes for that part of the story.

So the Foxes had, they said, formed a communications link with the dead – and soon numerous other people got into the act. Talkative, rapping poltergeists mushroomed all over the eastern seaboard of the USA in the next few years. And the Fox family, the mother and daughters, capitalised on their fame – staging large public shows, submitting to fairly rough and ready tests and examinations to prove their veracity. As their fame spread into a fad, the word 'spiritualism' was coined – and was instantly metamorphosed into a mass movement, a cult, a near-religion. In 1852, only four years after 'Mr Splitfoot' made contact with the Fox girls, the American spiritualist movement held a mass rally and convention in Cleveland. By then Europe had caught the infection, and was producing a few variations and additions to the themes.

Today the movement is worldwide, justifiably claiming millions of adherents, abundant in nearly every country. Hundreds of practitioners operate in nearly every sizeable city, and few small towns are without a 'medium' or two. (They are called mediums in the sense of 'middle-man', standing between the spirit world and the living.) Fifteen years ago, the number of spiritualists functioning in the USA was estimated at 150,000; there is no reason to assume that the number has declined since. In Britain, spiritualist meetings on a large public scale decorate Sunday evenings in most large centres, and about 200,000 people attend them regularly. Among occult beliefs and practices, perhaps only astrology can rival the spiritualist movement in size and international extent of belief.

But, necessarily, a book on revenants is no place to examine the rise of spiritualism as a worldwide movement. Our object must be to look at the basic activity on which the movement is based – the activity that, spiritualists claim, is no less than direct contact with the spirits of the departed. Once all the complications and window-dressings of the well-publicised cult have been peeled away, we are left with the basic pattern of the séance. In that process the medium – often a woman, but not always – enters the dissociated psychological state called a 'trance', during which time he or she becomes no more than a vehicle for the reception of spirit messages, and their transmission, in a variety of ways.

Obviously there is nothing new in that pattern. Think generally about men claiming to be in contact with the spirits, through trances, and the associations multiply: the oracles of ancient Greece, the 'possession' trances of Haitian voodoo, the 'demonic possession' that terrified the repressed convents and monasteries of medieval Europe, the 'speaking in tongues' of certain wild fundamentalist religions in present-day America – all the ecstatic states that fill up the history of man and his religions, primitive, ancient, and modern.

On a more specifically occult level, it seems that the Fox family and their poltergeist came along at precisely the right moment in a developing craze for 'psychic' matters, and shifted a bandwagon into top gear. We need only refer to the fame of Swedenborg, the 18th-century philosopher who is said to have had enormous psychic ability as a clairvoyant and communicator with spirits. Or, also in the 18th century, the man who spearheaded hypnotism – Anton Mesmer, with his 'animal magnetism' and his myriads of patients finding cures for nearly everything in their own individual hypnotic trances. Some of Mesmer's activities and followers may not have been entirely savoury, but his fame – and the hold he had on late 18th-century Europe – prepared the ground for the rise of other psychic sciences, and spiritualism.

It may be too glib to say that the 18th- and 19th-century emphases on rationalism and material virtues produced its counterweight in occult extravagances. Nevertheless, the rapid rise of spiritualism must one way or another prove that human society had created some array of needs that occultism was eager to answer; and that the world was ready for it when the Fox family, the first spiritualist mediums of the modern age, began chatting to a poltergeist.

Because the seeds of spiritualism were sown with that Arcadian 'rapping spirit', it is only just that other rappings and knockings should take first place in a quick survey of the *physical* phenomena of mediumship. But one must be careful not to think of the rappings as invariably the sound that knuckles make on wood. The spirits may now and then sound as if they are knocking on a door or politely rapping on a table for attention; but the noise can as easily range from a faint scratching or crackling to full-bodied booming sounds and ear-splitting detonations. Sir William Crookes, a scientist and leading British investigator of mediums in the last century, said that he had heard definite rapping noises coming from glass, from stretched wire, even from cloth. Other commentators have found that the noises can emanate from the empty air, which is as it should be if the rapping is being made by a spirit who is not limited to material necessities. Around the turn of the century, according to Hereward Carrington, another British psychical researcher of the time, an amateur 'psychic' frequently had the ability to produce *visible* rappings on the silk of an open umbrella. The indentations could clearly be seen, corresponding with each sound.

Few mediums, from the start of the movement, were

content with the limitations of rappings, coded for communication or not. The Fox girls and some of their earliest imitators soon introduced some variety into public séances, including the sound of invisible musical instruments, most usually guitars. A famous British medium of the 1870s and 1880s, William Stainton Moses, frequently produced musical sounds at his sittings – along with the usual assorted raps, and some special effects including brilliant, glowing lights, which were apparently at times accompanied by the rather giveaway odour of phosphorous smoke.

Self-starting music boxes seem to have been a favourite among mediums for decades, but accordions, flutes, and trumpets have also broken the breathless quiet of hundreds of séances. In 19th-century America, one Edward Childs seems to have made contact with a flute-playing spirit, while a thirteen-year-old would-be medium liked to spread out an array of instruments – accordion, triangle, tambourine, etc – and to invite the spirits in for a musical evening.

All these various noises, musical or otherwise, might have impressed many people in the early and fairly credulous days of spiritualism's audiences. But sophistication followed fast. More impressive proofs were needed of the presence of unseen spirits, and the mediums quickly provided them – often through the apparently miraculous movement of furniture. 'Table-turning' has since become a somewhat patronising synonym for séances, probably because it remains one of the most popular effects among 'physical' mediums.

Séances, of course, are generally held with the medium and her clients seated around a table, usually holding hands, and also usually in the dark. In the case of table-turning, though, the hands or fingertips of the 'sitters' may rest gently on the table top, which will make its uncanny movements under their lightest touch. A British psychical researcher, W. F. Barrett, described one sitting in which a heavy table 'sidled about', raised some or all of its legs off the floor and hung suspended, and finally made 'a series of very violent prancing movements' – which, afterwards, Barrett found himself unable to imitate by ordinary physical lifting.

Table movement also featured in the many remarkable phenomena apparently produced by the most famous British medium of all, Daniel Dunglas Home, whose success reached its peak in the mid-19th century. At a Home séance, a large mahogany table, on which rested loose articles like candles and a glass of water, tilted to an angle of more than thirty degrees off the horizontal: but none of the objects toppled from its position. Later, on that occasion, specific articles were made – on request – to slide off the tipped table, while the others stayed put.

Home, who claimed that his father was the illegitimate son of the tenth Earl of Home, picked up his spiritualist affiliations in the USA, during the wildfire spread of the Foxes' fame. His physical mediumship gained worldwide notice, and came to be thoroughly investigated by an assortment of researchers and amateur experts. Though his séances were alive with all the phenomena so far mentioned – ghostly music and lights, rappings and table shiftings – he remains best remembered for another feat. It was seen in Chapter Four that poltergeists sometimes abandoned the joys of throwing objects about, and turned to throwing, or lifting, people – an activity, in spiritualism, given the term 'levitation'. Home was a great levitator – rising into the air and being suspended there for minutes at a time, as a regular feature of his séances.

Other mediums before and since have demonstrated levitation, but it would seem none so resoundingly as Home, especially on a night in 1868, when in the view of three reliable witnesses Home floated out of one window of a London house and in again at another. The windows were said to be eighty feet from the ground; and there were no ledges or other footholds linking the two.

All the weird effects mentioned so far served ideally to convince mediums' clients that the spirits were making their presence felt, and/or that psychic forces were at work. But they were all fairly unwieldy means for direct communication – and so techniques evolved (still in the realm of physical phenomena) to open channels for more explicit messages from beyond. One method, common today among amateur mediums, requires the laying out of the letters of the alphabet in a circle on the table; in the centre, a drinking glass or similar object is placed, with the medium and the sitters perhaps each resting a finger lightly on the glass. Under the influence of the spirits, or whatever, the glass moves from letter to letter, spelling out the alphabet.

Then there is the ouija board (its name is an amalgam of the French and German for 'yes'), also based on the alphabetical principle, with a pointer sliding round the board; the medium's hand or fingertips may rest lightly on the pointer. The ouija board held a dominant position among do-it-yourself spiritualists earlier in this century, combining an element of occultism with the fun of a parlour game. As the late 1960s have brought another fad for the supernatural to sweep the western world, sales of the boards have reached new heights.

Building up words from the alphabet perhaps proves laborious, so mediums have sometimes invited the spirits to do their own writing. 'Automatic' writing, as it is called, occurs when the medium enters the receptive state holding a pencil or pen in a position that would seem to limit his or her own transcriptive ability – in the left hand, say, if the medium is right-handed, or between two middle fingers, hardly gripping it at all. As if of its own volition, the pencil will begin to write as readily as tables will turn. Sometimes, though, the writing is indecipherable scribbling (when the usual explanation is 'poor vibrations', like static on a radio receiver, or perhaps the intervention of evil, mischievous spirits). Occasionally the writing, as script, will be clear, but meaningless, though meanings can usually be pried from such messages by assiduous 'interpretation'.

To simplify automatic writing, the *planchette* was invented in France in the 19th century, consisting of a little platform on castors, with a pencil attached. The medium's hand or fingertips rested on the platform, and it scurried around on its wheels writing out messages. Like the ouija board, the planchette seems to have recently come in for a new spate of popularity.

Spiritualists have made some incredible claims for automatic writing, which remains one of the most interesting of the physical phenomena of the séance. In 1913 Mrs Pearl Curran, a middle-aged American lady whose life had until then been in no way extraordinary, took up the ouija and shortly found herself in communication with the 'spirit' of a 17th-century girl named Patience Worth. Through automatic writing (and later through dictation from the lips of Mrs Curran, in trance) Patience wrote numerous poems, essays and novels – the latter, especially, showing a broad and detailed knowledge of 17th-century life. At least one expert has pointed out that the 17th-century dialect used in her novel *Telka* is authentic, and startlingly free from anachronisms.

Earlier, in the years immediately after 1901, a scattering of mediums at various places round the world began picking up spirit messages (through automatic writing) that seemed curiously linked. Apparently the great British psychical researcher, F. W. H. Myers, had announced (before his death) his intention of proving survival if possible by communicating after he had died. Myers died in 1901; the messages bore a number of 'cross-correspondences', as the SPR came to call them, which seemed to prove to many people's satisfaction that Myers had been able to get some words back across the barrier.

From fairly recent years, there was the case of Miss Geraldine Cummins, British author of some sixteen books written by automatic writing, at the rate of 2,000 words an hour. (Two of these, incidentally, are said to have been dictated by Myers.) In the 1950s an English woman named Miss Grace Rosher took down messages from her dead fiancé – with a pen merely resting on the top of her index finger. She also wrote messages said to emanate from the spirit of another distinguished psychical researcher, Sir William Crookes. Recently some highly sceptical journalists watched her in action, finding that – aside from the content or supposed authors of the messages – the fact that the pen wrote at all, in that position, was eerie enough.

Finally, in the late 1960s, a lady named Rosemary Brown startled London by producing manuscripts of original music which she said had been dictated to her by Liszt, Schubert, Beethoven, and other great dead composers. Though she had taken piano lessons in her time, and had an interest in classical music, she had had no formal training in composition or musicology. Yet various experts found the music she produced to be remarkably akin to that of the dead composers – even seeming to show, in some instances, that the composers' work had progressed or developed, along quite likely lines. Interestingly, Rosemary Brown never entered trance, but received musical dictation in full consciousness.

Less verbally inclined spirits often choose to manifest themselves in extremely concrete physical ways, such as the production out of nowhere of 'apports', a term introduced in the previous chapter with regard to spontaneous poltergeists. In the late 19th century a British medium named Mrs Samuel Guppy achieved fame through the production at her séances of quantities of flowers. One such bouquet of apports was described (by the naturalist A. R. Wallace, then investigating spiritualism) as half covering the table, 'flowers and fern leaves, all fresh, cold and damp with dew ... ordinary winter flowers, which are cultivated in hothouses for table decoration, the stems apparently cut off as if for a bouquet'. Mme Elisabeth d'Esperant, a medium of early 20th-century France, seems also to have been given to producing flowers – including a golden lily some seven feet tall.

Most spiritualists tend to use the word 'materialisation' as partial explanation of the source of these apports – but the term comes in for more use with regard to the solid, three-dimensional manifestation of the spirits themselves, through the psychically powerful agency of the medium. When materialisation occurs, the mediums assert that the spirits, the revenants, are entirely there – flesh and blood, dressed sometimes in normal clothes, but more often in predictably spiritual flowing robes. Sometimes, of course, the materialisation is incomplete – a face, a head and shoulders, a functioning spirit hand.

Materialisation occurred early in the history of the movement: in 1860 one of the Fox sisters supposedly brought about the appearance of a 'luminous' female figure that walked about the séance room. In the 1870s a young medium named Florence Cook materialised a ghostly face, and later a complete figure – which was seen by witnesses in a good light, photographed, conversed with, and touched.

Almost invariably, the spirits are said to materialise by means of a substance known as 'ectoplasm', apparently an invisible and 'etheric' variant on protoplasm. Ectoplasm is supposedly present in the living human body, and is capable of solidifying and becoming visible when extruded from the medium's pores and orifices. It is the clay, as it were, from which the spirit moulds itself a temporary body. In 1953, in Pennsylvania, USA, a medium entered trance inside a curtained cabinet in full view of some eighty people at a public meeting – who all later claimed to have seen a spirit materialisation from a smoky white cloud of ectoplasm. Infra-red photographs captured the event on film – though without managing to distinguish satisfactorily the exact nature of that smoky white cloud.

We will come back to look again, perhaps more critically, at the physical phenomena of mediumship that have been catalogued. But first it is necessary to add to this survey of spiritualist phenomena the *mental,* or purely psychic, kind. And dominant among those phenomena is the most common activity of mediums everywhere – the spoken messages from the dead, wherein (the theory says) the spirit takes over the entranced medium, using his or her mouth and vocalising apparatus to speak its words, often in its own voice. Take, for example, the case of a Scottish medium of the 1860s, David Duguid, who was apparently 'possessed' in this way by the spirit of a Persian prince 2,000 years dead. Through Duguid's lips the prince delivered himself of many historical discourses (correcting a few 'errors' in the history books) and a few homilies about the wonders of the afterlife.

One of the best known deliverers of spirit (spoken) messages was Mrs Leonora Piper, a 19th-century American trance medium, who became the subject of many intensive studies by psychical researchers. She made frequent vocal contact with the spirits of her relatives, and at other times provided 'sitters' with messages from *their* relatives. In one instance, she provided a leading British scientist with a message from his dead uncle, containing such specific and intimate detail as to satisfy the scientist of the authenticity.

Trance mediums who speak for the spirits often tend to be 'possessed' regularly by one spirit – their spirit guide or 'control' – so that there are *two* go-betweens setting up communication to a living client from whatever dead person the client wishes to contact. That is, the spirit guide passes on, second-hand, through the medium's lips, the messages from your dead Aunt Alice or Uncle George. Often the guides have exotic, rather outlandish names and natures: many American mediums and a fair number of British ones seem to be 'controlled' by the shades of dead American Indian chiefs. Others are more ordinary, like 'Feda', the spirit of a six-year-old girl who was said to have acted as the control of a modern British medium, Mrs Osborne Leonard. Like other such controls, Feda sometimes spoke on behalf of other spirits, sometimes merely introduced them before stepping aside to let the others 'possess' Mrs Leonard and speak for themselves.

With mediums through whom the spirits speak, we come to tread in a gingerly fashion on the edge of that *terra incognita* called extra-sensory perception. Certainly we plunge deeper into it with those mediums who deliver their spirit messages first-hand, *not* when in the trance state. These are the clairvoyants (or clairaudiants, who hear rather than see the invisible spirits), and their numbers are legion. Perhaps most numerous are the kind that stage large public meetings, at which they will produce snippets of 'spirit messages', find someone in the audience who feels a snippet applies to him, and follow it up with other fragments that purport to be a message for that person from the dead. Often the message has no real informational content: it seems that in these instances the spirit is merely making itself known to the person in the audience, and trying to prove its identity – by dredging up details of its past life, or the living person's life, that would be unknown to a stranger.

Again we will return to this aspect of spiritualism, and

the relationship between the dead and ESP. Finally, in this nutshell survey of the work of a medium, we must glance briefly at the process known as 'spirit healing'. If *faith* healing demands that the healer's psychic powers, or whatever, are focused on medical problems, then spirit healing demands the same focus of the powers of spirit guides. Through the medium – who need not be a trance medium – the spirit provides diagnosis and cure. In modern Brazil, a country where spiritualism has a firm status, many hospitals and clinics are operated by spirit-ualist societies, and the spirits even sometimes choose the doctors to staff them. In modern Britain, according to a British apologist for spiritualism, Maurice Barbinell, a few mediums can actually manage 'psychic surgery' – including the removal of internal growths and so on, by 'spirit power', without opening the body or doing more than merely touching the affected area. Sometimes, indeed, even the touch is apparently unnecessary, for Mr Barbinell gives (in his book *Spiritualism Today*, 1969) examples of healing at a distance.

Any discussion of spiritualism and mediumship must necessarily come round to the obvious questions: is it true, does it work, is there proof? Or can it all be shown to be fraud and trickery, at varying degrees of complexity, in which – to adapt McLuhan's aphorism – the medium turns out after all to be the message?

A near lifetime of study would be required, to sift all the documentation and evidence and reports of investiga-tions, before an opinion could be fairly formed. A great many large and impressive volumes have emerged out of just such detailed study – and we can do little more here than refer to some of those volumes, pro and con, and hint at the conclusions reached in them. If the reader is still dissatisfied, he must conduct his own investigations – if he can find a medium or two willing to be investigated.

First of all, it must be stressed that the opportunities for fraud, in séances, are nearly infinite. And it follows that a great many people have taken advantage of those opportunities, because of the equally large opportunities for profit that spiritualism offers. The world abounds in gullible people, and in the confidence men who prey on them; and the latter readily find their way into occultism as into other fields. Many writers have devoted books to exposing the likelihood of fraud; many investigators have devoted their time to exposing charlatans in action. For the former, one might look at Hereward Carrington's *The Physical Phenomena of Spiritualism*, with its delightful details of how to turn tables or make rapping noises without being detected, and other marvels. Less well known is a book by America's John Mulholland, *Beware Familiar Spirits*, equally full of fascinating information about séance trickery: tables made with hidden rapping or turning mechanisms, proof against any search short of taking them apart; techniques for automatic writing effects, the use of muslin and other materials for ectoplasmic materialisations, and so on.

Mulholland makes the point (nor is he alone in stressing it) that people generally see what they want to see, or expect to see – and that any ordinary stage magician or conjuror, having properly primed his audience, could fairly readily produce the physical phenomena of spiritualism. In fact, many such conjurors have turned to mediumship, as more lucrative than stage magic. But the greatest conjuror of all, Harry Houdini, utilised his talents and vast knowledge of the field in a one-man investigation of mediums that turned up many such tricksters. Houdini was a member of a committee set up in 1923 by the magazine *Scientific American*, which offered $5,000 to any medium who could satisfy the committee that the phenomena he or she produced were not faked. In the end, no one won the money. Houdini, the escape artist, thwarted one medium who offered to produce phenomena while thoroughly tied up. Apparently that medium had always been able to slip his bonds, but he failed to get out of the involved bondage that Houdini imposed on him – and so no phenomena were manifested. (Incidentally, some years ago the British SPR made a similar offer – £250 to any *physical* medium who would allow an infra-red camera to probe the usual darkness at a séance. Apparently the offer was never taken up.)

It might seem that trance mediumship, and the clair-voyant kind of spirit contact, would be the easiest to fake. But remember that the *mental* phenomena of spiritualism require the delivery of messages that will convince an audience of the identity of the communicating spirit – whereas the physical phenomena (other than automatic writing) serve to convince the audience merely that there are spirits present. Still, since about nine-tenths of an audience is eager to be convinced, messages can come easily from the fraudulent mediums. Generally, the char-latans begin a line of patter with vague and generalised references, watching their audience for flickers of interest, fishing hard, and picking up quickly on any connections they might make. This process holds especially true in the large public spiritualist meetings. Katharine Whitehorn, the British journalist, described one such meeting in 1960 where, for example, the medium asked a man in the audience if a particular name meant anything to him. The man, who was French, replied that he spoke little English; without hesitation, the medium produced the name 'Lebrun' – did that call up a memory, she asked? An old friend, perhaps? Something from the war?

Transcribed as baldly as that, the technique seems obvious and full of holes. But in the hectic atmosphere of the meeting, it would not be so readily seen through; people would be ready, fully primed, for a name or phrase that would strike a chord, however distant or vague or generalised that chord might be.

In the dim and intimate atmosphere of the smaller séance, the same techniques can be used: rapid-fire patter and conversation, plenty of fishing and probing for reactions, the trained skills of the false medium following up the reactions till more and more detail emerges – without the client realising that he is giving himself away. Dr D. J. West, in his book *Psychical Research Today*, refers to the 'innumerable small indications' that act as give-aways: 'a little extra movement, a change in breathing, will all serve to let the medium know that she is on the right track'.

Of course, the tricks of the trade need not always rely on this highly skilled instant probing. Cases of fraudulent mediums include those who engage in extensive pre-séance research into the lives of their prospective clients, so as to produce 'unknown' information out of their faked clairvoyant visions. One modern medium is said to have asked clients to leave handbags, briefcases and other personal property in another room – saying that such objects interfered with the vibrations. Then while the medium was warming up in the early stages of the séance, an accomplice would ransack the possessions for intimate information about the clients.

On the other hand, many trance mediums are certainly not confidence tricksters, but do undeniably enter a trance state from which automatic writing, or speech in strange voices, issues forth. A 19th-century American medium, Ada Bessinet, thoroughly investigated by psychical researchers, was found definitely to enter a trance, and so was cleared of any imputation of conscious fraud. But the investigators suggested that she was *unconsciously* producing the spirit messages, that they were coming from a 'secondary personality' released by the trance.

One of the most famous, and deservedly so, modern

mediums has been America's Eileen Garrett, who later
gave up her practice to launch a Parapsychology Foundation. In her autobiography, *Many Voices*, she turns aside
from a consideration of survival after death, and outlines
her belief that the spirit guides and so on are 'principals
of the subconscious' – or, as she otherwise puts it, 'working
symbols' of the subconscious. That is, while she sees them
as entities in their own right, she does not see them as
revenants. Nor, however, does she see them as necessarily
schizoid personalities split (in a psychotic way) off from
the medium's primary self. She feels that they are 'formed
from spiritual and emotional needs of the person involved', but she realises that – as with the controversial
subject of ESP – modern research has barely begun to
explore these aspects of man's psychic makeup, and has
certainly not yet produced any answers.

If the foregoing glimpse of conscious and unconscious
trickery puts a heavy strain on the credibility of spiritualism, we must nevertheless remember – as many distinguished investigators would remind us – that the
existence of a white crow or two is still possible, however
many black ones have been seen. The best and most reliable investigators are those whose approach is based on a
healthy scientific open-mindedness. And many of them
have come across achievements by mediums that seem
almost wholly inexplicable – certainly not fraud, conscious
or otherwise, and also hard to explain in terms of those
cloudy concepts lumped together as ESP. Mrs Garrett herself produced one of the more famous, in 1930, when she
apparently made contact with the spirit of the pilot of a
great dirigible that had crashed disastrously two days
earlier. There had been no prior intention to seek information about the crash; it emerged spontaneously at the
sitting, when the alleged spirit of the pilot gave a detailed
rundown of the causes of the crash. The details received

by Mrs Garrett were mostly borne out, in fine detail, at the official inquiry into the crash held some time later.

So the work and writings of the rare individuals like Eileen Garrett provide the opposite side of the picture to that of sham and deception. And any layman, digging round in the mountains of material on the subject, will undoubtedly turn up other cases in which – at the very least – the medium's achievement cannot be dismissed out of hand, beyond a reasonable doubt. As one final example, consider the case of the late James A. Pike, once Bishop of California, who – after the death of his son – became deeply involved with spiritualism when some spontaneous phenomena seemed to indicate the possibility of survival after death, and messages from the dead.

Bishop Pike was no hysteric, no crank, certainly no fraud. In his writings, interviews, and television appearances (including televised séances that startled the nation), he seemed to be very simply an honest man confronting a complex and disturbing mystery. Not everyone would agree that a mystery truly exists. Certainly not everyone would accept the answers that the bishop came up with. But, just as certainly, a great number of people – from the anxious and gullible seekers of reassurance about death, to the scrupulously scientific psychical investigators – are going to go on asking the questions.

6

Inhuman Phantoms

6

Inhuman Phantoms

ONE feature of apparitions of the dead can be found constantly recurring in almost all instances, as it recurs in Chapter Three of this book, but is seldom singled out as especially remarkable. It is that apparitional revenants generally appear *clothed*. Their garments may well be only winding sheets, or the flowing ethereal robes of spiritualist manifestations; but when the figure of a ghost is fully visible, it is also fully dressed. Moreover, many ghosts bear with them certain objects from which they may have been inseparable in life: the drummer has his drum, the soldier has his rifle or sword, the Scots piper has his pipes, the murderer re-enacting the crime has his weapon.

Now without venturing too far into a sticky and inconclusive discussion of the nature of the soul, we must find it a fair strain on our credulity to believe that these inanimate objects can return from the dead. If ghosts are visible human *spirits*, why should the spirit be fully accoutred in the clothing and possessions that encumbered the flesh? Consider the British businessman in recent years who saw a ghostly band of Roman soldiers encamped in some woods one night. He knew they were ghosts because he could see through them – armour, helmets, and all. And Chapter Three mentioned the haunt of a clergyman in a London church, which the vicar of the church walked through one day. So the haunt's garments were as unsubstantial, apparitional, as the rest of him.

The difficulty tends to throw something of a shadow on any ideas about ghosts in terms of survival after death. Of course, primitive peoples and some ancient cultures placed favourite possessions into graves with the deceased, on the presumed principle that these objects – or, perhaps, their non-physical 'essences' – would accompany the dead man into the afterlife. But can we really think, today, in terms of the ghostly essence of a suit of clothes, or a Roman sword, returning with their owners from beyond the grave? Instead, the reports of spectral clothing and other articles seem to lend weight to the idea that apparitions are hallucinations of one kind or another. If one is going to conjure up in the mind's eye the image of a spectral grey lady or whatever, one might as well observe the proprieties and ensure that the hallucination is adequately clothed, as ghosts in folklore always have been.

And by the same token, if one allows the range of the human hallucinatory ability to be stretched a trifle, it is no great effort to include apparitions of a great many inanimate objects in their own right, with human spectres either absent or in subsidiary roles. Certain of these objects recur again and again in ghost tales the world over, and among them one motif that occurs with striking frequency is the ghostly *light*.

In the old days, the greatest number of inexplicable lights would have been ascribed to some legendary spirit like Britain's Will o' the Wisp (known also as Jack O'Lantern, under which name he was exported to America). Will, or Jack, was originally a kind of nature spirit, an 'elemental' – not the ghost of a dead person but a supernatural being who never had been human. He took particular pleasure in leading people astray over marshes and bogs (for, of course, his origin can largely be found in the eerie but natural phosphorescence that marshland often produces). But he rapidly found his way into ghost

legend – since such phosphorescence can now and then be
seen over graveyards as well.

Associated with Will o' the Wisp is the prevalent myth
of the 'corpse candle', an inexplicable light that tends to
hover over the place where an unburied corpse lies – as if
to guide searchers. One such hovered near an old Welsh
chapel, according to a 19th-century story, and later at the
same spot a ploughman unearthed some human bones that
were thought to be the remains of a murdered man.
Corpse candles occur frequently in tales concerning
searches for victims of drowning; clearly the lights are
thought to be some manifestation of the dead person's
spirit, seeking (as ghosts so often do) to get its body
properly buried. An old West of England belief explicitly
states that weird lights flickering along coastlines were the
ghosts of drowned sailors, dead without proper rites, and
so condemned to eternal restlessness.

Phantom lights like those just mentioned seem in a
way to be substitutes for the human-figure type of ghost,
as does the light in a 19th-century tale from North Carolina, USA, concerning a railwayman who was decapitated
in an accident. The stretch of track where the tragedy
happened was haunted by a moving light – which, the
story says, was the dead man's head eternally searching for
his body. But sometimes lights occur as part of a generalised haunting, with no specific reference to a dead person
or a past disaster. Borley Rectory's many haunts including
weird lights at empty windows, as also occurred in a
famous haunted house in Maine, USA. Near Taunton,
Somerset, a deserted and haunted house was said to con-
tain one room that always emitted a chilling green-blue
light. And the British writer Dennis Bardens mentions a
few accounts from recent years of inexplicable lights visiting people in Britain – including one case in Sunderland
when the light floated silently through a wall.

That Sunderland light, and many other ghost lights, was a beautiful ethereal blue (which, in symbolism, was always the colour of spirituality). But a few phantom lights have shone a fiery red – like a 19th-century flaming light that frequently shone *out* of a barn near the English town of Hollinwood. At first everyone thought the barn was on fire, but when they went inside the barn, everything was normal. A comparable story from the USA tells of a North Carolina plantation home that suddenly seemed to light up as if aflame one night – though the red glare vanished when onlookers came near to the house. The next day a message arrived to say that the daughter of the house, living abroad, had died, at the same time as the ghostly flare.

Ghost lights can often be omens of death as well as announcements. The Highlands of Scotland have produced a legion of tales about such luminous warnings, which may spring up well in advance of a death or during the last hours of a dying person. The theme is universal, and includes the death omens that used to be read in the appearance of meteorites (falling stars) – though today people may more readily see such phenomena as UFOs than morbid forewarnings. More explicitly presaging death were the five lights seen last century in a Welsh mansion in Carmarthenshire, some months before five servants were suffocated in the house by fumes from a coal fire. And from America comes a tale of a haunted region in rural North Carolina, where processions of lights – sometimes thought to be the ghosts of long-dead Indians – weave through the woods during any night when a local person dies.

Most of these spectral lights might well be related to some longstanding notions about the 'luminosity' of the human spirit, as with the haloes of holy people and saints, or the glowing ethereal 'auras' that many clairvoyants and spiritualists claim to see surrounding every living person.

So it is not at all unacceptable, in terms of ghost lore, that revenants might take this form. But it may seem a little more unacceptable that hauntings should take the form, as many do, of ineradicable bloodstains. Blood is hardly something emitted by our spiritual beings. Yet remember the highly charged symbolism of blood alluded to in Chapter Two: if 'the blood is the life', perhaps it can be the ghost as well.

Bloodstain haunts have much in common with the ghosts who re-enact their deaths. So they usually appear to mark the place of a killing. In County Clare, Ireland, a woman in a haunted house was mysteriously killed – by the ghosts, it was said – and thereafter left her own ghostly mark in a recurring bloodstain on the wall. In Hampden House, a great stately home in Oxfordshire, one room is supposedly marked with such stains where a lord of the manor was executed centuries ago. And a tavern in 19th-century Massachusetts, USA, had such stains on a staircase where the owner had murdered and robbed a traveller.

The ghostly blood of murder victims does not only stain the woodwork of old houses. The American folk-lorist Richard M. Dorson mentions blood that sullied, each year, the fruit of an apple tree beneath which a murder had been committed in 17th-century Connecticut. Blood also reddened a Maine beach where one 18th-century winter the crew of a wrecked ship died, and stained a patch of moss elsewhere in Maine, where a brutal Indian massacre once occurred. Finally, mention must be made of a widespread folktale motif in which a stonemason jealously kills a talented apprentice who has designed a beautiful cathedral window. Unremovable blood stains the window in the legend – which has been applied to Lincolnshire Cathedral, Rouen Cathedral, and many other churches and abbeys.

With bloodstains, we have not moved too far from the

humanoid kind of phantoms. But ghost lore is filled with tales of wholly inanimate objects returning with, as it were, an afterlife of their own. These must not be confused with 'haunted' objects that move about under some uncanny influence; such matters are variants on poltergeist activity. When a portion of a house is seen – from a distance – to have collapsed, but is perfectly intact on closer examination (as in a tale from New England), that is either witchery or delusion, but it is not a spectral house. But America has produced such a house, in one instance of the 'vanishing hitchhiker' theme outlined in Chapter Three. The girl hitchhiker took the car owners home with her, and gave them a good dinner in a well furnished and tastefully decorated house. About a month later the driver of the car passed that way again, and found that the house was boarded up and visibly deteriorating. Some local people informed him that the house had been left like that when its owner, whose description was that of the hitchhiker, had died – two *years* previously.

Much ghost lore seems to have grown up around various means of transport though, as yet, not too many worthwhile tales of spectral cars or jet planes have been disseminated. There was a ghostly bus, however, which frightened a number of people in London in 1934. It rushed along the streets at night with all its lights on, but without passengers, conductor, or driver. And railway legends include quite a few good ghost-train stories; many of them, like a 19th-century case in Colorado, regularly re-enact the tragedy of a train wreck. And people near a railway line out of Boston often hear at night the rushing approach of a locomotive and train, but nothing appears.

Also from the USA comes a famous legend of the funeral train carrying the coffin of Abraham Lincoln, which is said to repeat its run along a stretch of track in New York state every April. Aside from the murdered president, it carries a spectral military band, visibly playing though no music can be heard.

Men have been seafarers longer than railroaders, and the tales of phantom ships vastly outnumber ghost trains. Everyone has probably heard of the prototype, the *Flying Dutchman*. Its story has many variations, but basically it is said that the captain committed some crime – usually a sacrilege against God or against some spirit of the sea – and was condemned forever to sail the seas without putting into port. It is most usually seen off the Cape of Good Hope, either during the storms that so often lash that region, or as a forewarning of storms. A French ship named *La Belle Rosalie* apparently haunts the seas in a similar fashion.

Other ghostly vessels bring some unique features to the theme. The good ship *Palatine*, in the 18th century, was abandoned (with passengers) by a mutinous crew and later enticed onto a rocky American coast by wreckers; it re-enacts the wreck each year, always with the accompaniment of chilling screams from the ghosts of those who died on her. An American ship named *Dash* vanished at sea, but its phantom returns to port now and then, to pick up the ghosts of relatives of the crew.

Pirate ships seem as unable to rest as their evil masters: Captain Kidd's vessel often sails into New England coves to ensure that the pirate's treasure remains safely buried; and Lafitte's ship has been sighted near Galveston, Texas, where it was supposedly sunk in the 1820s. Sometimes seekers after pirate treasure watch for such ships, and later dig over the beaches where they seem to anchor – as did a man earlier in this century on the Massachusetts coast. But, as Richard Dorson tells it, he found only clamshells. Another *Dutchman*-like ship, named the *Cameo*, plies the seas off the west coast of the USA, bearing a horde of gold seekers forever searching for the mythical gold-rich Bay of Trinidad.

A schooner wrecked by a storm on Lake Erie, off the Canadian shore, is said to reappear before other dangerous storms, and on Lake Erie a phantom steamship was seen – in flames – in the 1860s. Oddly, another ghostly steamboat occurs on remote Devil's Lake in North Dakota, though no one seems to know what past event it mirrors. Even more oddly, phantom ships have been seen sailing majestically through the air – off a west of England coastline in the 18th century, and over the waterless Colorado desert in the 1870s. And, just to bring the theme more up to date, a US Navy officer recently wrote an account of two phantom sailing ships seen by himself and some shipmates, off the California coast, during World War Two. Other crew members found it hard to believe, for nothing had registered on the radar.

Of all ghostly modes of transport, the old-fashioned horse-drawn vehicle has come in for literally the longest run. One phantom coach, recurring in Lincolnshire, apparently rumbles along by itself, with no visible means of propulsion; but others generally have a full complement of spectral horses, not to mention drivers and occasionally even passengers. With the mention of horses, of course, we begin to enter the area of ghost animals, a concept we may find slightly easier to swallow – in terms of spirits returning from the dead – than ghostly objects. After all, most animal lovers insist that at least the higher animals ought to be considered to have souls – and so they should have ghosts. Soulless *coaches* appearing as revenants are something else again; but they and their horses can rarely be separated.

In some stories of ghostly coaches, the drivers have the principal roles; the coaches are merely props, addenda. Like the wicked Lord Lonsdale of 18th-century Britain, who terrorised his house and estate after death, and was sometimes seen abroad in a coach and six. The ghost of a noble lady in Worcestershire drove a coach and four through the rooms of a country house, though sometimes she changed direction and drove into the moat, which invariably bubbled and steamed. By contrast, the ghost of a Shropshire squire usually appeared by *emerging* from water – a local pool – and was given to driving his coach and four white horses into the dining room of his home. And poor Anne Boleyn's father, Sir Thomas, underlined that family's ill luck by being condemned – for some unknown reason – eternally to drive a coach over forty bridges pursued by shrieking fiends.

In other hauntings, the identity of the driver seems less important, or at least less well known – as with the ghostly coach that draws up before an Essex mansion, every New Year's Eve, to set down a ghostly lady, who is admitted to the house by a ghostly butler. Cornwall had a regular haunting ghost driving a black coach, with no particular legend attached to it. But its special feature, which occurs in many coach legends, shows in the fact that the horses were headless.

Now we saw in Chapter Three that many legendary human apparitions have been headless, mostly because their living originals were executed by decapitation. But why should teams of horses lack heads? In the absence of a certain explanation, one must assume that the headlessness – which often extends to the unknown drivers of phantom coaches – is merely a refinement added to a ghost story for the sake of extra shivers. And also, possibly, to ensure that no one can accuse the teller of the tale of having mistaken a real coach for a spectral one. So the ghost of an Irish family consists of a vast plumed carriage with, as Elliott O'Donnell tells it, headless horses; and in Doneraile a phantom coach with headless driver and horses terrified the populace with a special trick – knocking on doors and flinging human blood at anyone who dared to answer.

Such ghosts are plentiful in Ireland, where – as in many

other places – they are often attached to certain families, and serve as death omens, or as 'fetches' arriving while someone is dying. One such coach (with headless horses) that appears to a Limerick family when a member of it is dying, is said always to be filled with the ghosts of family ancestors – who have left only one empty seat. And a modern writer in *Fate* magazine recalls his own experience, in Somerset in 1905, when a spectral coach pulled up to his family's house some hours before his mother died. The horses had heads in that case, but the driver had the face of a skeleton.

Horses come in for a good deal of ghost activity when out of harness and under saddle: mention was made in Chapter Three of the widespread myth of the 'wild hunt', led by many different legendary heroes but usually involving spectral horses. Sir Francis Drake himself has been adopted, in Devon legend, as leader of a local wild hunt. Chapter Three also mentioned the common motif of the headless horseman, which Washington Irving borrowed for his classic story; but other ghostly horsemen may appear intact. A rider in Lancashire recurs every year, galloping up to a local mansion and going inside to re-enact a 17th-century murder. Dick Turpin, the famous British highwayman, is said to haunt many different stretches of road across England, and so needs still to be mounted. A 19th-century phantom horseman appeared to a traveller in Wales just in time to save the traveller from attack by a dangerous robber. In 1906 a rider met with a fatal accident, and the horse had to be destroyed soon after: at the moment when it was killed, a friend saw both horse and rider galloping along a road nearby. And a well-dressed man on a spirited horse has been seen fairly recently riding on a road in Kent, seeming quite ordinary and lifelike (especially when manifest in daylight) but having an unsettling tendency to vanish suddenly.

Because of all the spectral coaches and ghostly riders,

horses tend to get an extra large share of the number of ghosts stories involving animals. But there are comparatively few cases of ghost horses on their own. Glamorgan, in South Wales, has known a white horse that haunted a churchyard and seemed to prefer walking on its hind legs; and another white horse, huge and luminous, was seen by Elliott O'Donnell on an estate in the Chilterns. A Shropshire man who robbed a grave was haunted by the disturbed occupant, who inexplicably chose to appear as a colt.

Sometimes the ghostly horses are heard but not seen: like the invisible ghost of an Irish suicide, riding an unseen horse whose legendary hoofbeats have been heard near Monagh. And not too many years ago in the west of England a traveller heard hoofbeats one night in a field, though moonlight revealed it to be wholly empty. As with the ghost coaches, the lone ghost horses can sometimes presage disaster – a superstition especially prevalent among miners. So a spectral pit pony sometimes appears in a Durham coal mine as a bad-luck omen, as does a great white horse in a Utah silver mine – though the latter has been seen in the shape of a mule, and occasionally as a headless mule.

Only rarely does a ghostly horse appear to do good: Eric Maple recalls one modern anecdote, when a pet horse returned from the dead to drive a robber away from its mistress. But in past centuries horses were seldom pets; the role of protective animal ghosts is generally left to the dog, who also – predictably – claim the largest number of ghost stories involving animals on their own.

Stories of protective doggy ghosts include a tale from old Wales of a woman who often walked the mountain roads to village markets, but who was caught on those lonely paths one night, in terror of wild animals. Then from nowhere came a huge, friendly, white dog, who walked beside her until they reached her cottage – when it disappeared. Throughout Britain, numerous ghostly dogs (usually black) serve as traditional guardians of ancient stately homes. And most authorities agree that these animals are probably adaptations of much older elemental nature spirits (many of which were kindly disposed), recently domesticated into canine ghosts. Then again, in the cruel old days, builders of castles and mansions would sometimes bury an animal alive in the walls, just to create such a protective ghost – though why the spectral dog would willingly perform this service, after such barbaric treatment, is difficult to understand.

These guardian spirits are usually black dogs, and are most prevalent in East Anglia. That area, too, is the home of the 'black shuck' (or 'barquest'), a dangerous ghost dog that has been said to attack people, and to be a general death omen. Some descriptions of him assert that he is of a species of hound now extinct in England; others add to his horror by endowing him with only one eye, glowing ferally. The shuck has counterparts in legends of black dogs from other localities: the 'boggart' of Lancashire is another famous revenant, though that county also boasts a spectral dog variously called the 'shriker' or 'trash', sometimes a death omen too, but according to one tale given to a few good works, like frightening a compulsive gambler into giving up gambling. Another kindly black dog, from Dorset folklore, came regularly to sit by a farmhouse fire until the exasperated farmer once chased it out of the house. But it exited through the roof, and near the hole it made the farmer found some hidden money.

Other famous black dogs include the 'gwyllgi' of Wales (though some versions describe it as spotted); the spaniel-like 'Manthe dog' that haunts – in a friendly fashion – Peel Castle on the Isle of Man; another harmless canine of an aristocratic house in County Clare, Ireland; a black Labrador, once mistreated and killed by sailors on a Lake

Erie vessel, said to haunt that vessel ever since. Ghostly black dogs have also been seen in fairly recent years in Hertfordshire, in Bristol, in Edinburgh, and in 1958 in Essex.

But then ghost dogs can come in all colours and breeds. In 19th-century West Virginia the ghost of a Negro woman slave, killed by her master, haunted the man to death – in the shape of a white dog. A grey dog accompanied a faceless human apparition in its haunting of a Birmingham (England) house in the 1880s; the ghost of a pet dachshund visited its owner in London early in the 20th century; while in the 18th century an Oxford college was plagued by the appearance of a large, yellow, phantom dog.

Dogs necessarily feature in the myth of the wild hunt, and are then usually monstrous hounds with demonic glowing eyes (a feature shared by some of the best known haunting dogs). A huntsman and a pack of hounds gallop over Warwickshire fields every Christmas Eve, and another demonic hunt with fearsome hounds comes from the folklore of Cornwall. An anecdote from the 1800s concerns an officer in the Duke of Wellington's army who took along a pack of hounds to occupy his leisure time with hunting; his ghost and those of the dogs still hunt, in local legend, over the Spanish countryside.

The foregoing is merely a minute sampling of all the available ghost-dog legends, which deserve, and could fill, a large book to themselves. With other animals, the stories become noticeably fewer. Even the cat, with all its supernatural associations, seems to have little place in ghost legends, either because its traditional nine lives tend to forestall its transformation into a ghost, or more probably because cats – as witches' familiars and so on – tend to be seen as disguised demons rather than mere apparitions. Anyway, of the few cat phantoms available, one might mention the oversized white cat that haunts a road in Lincolnshire – once seen during a snowfall, when it left no prints.

If cats are recognised as ghosts, folklore generally prefers to consider them the ghosts of dead witches – though one cat that haunted a house in the north of England convinced the owner that it was the ghost of her deceased mother. A well-disposed cat ghost in old Virginia lore, probably a deceased witch, once helped a poor Negro to find some buried treasure. Rather more unhappy cat ghosts include one that re-enacts its death by torture in an Oxenby manor house, and a headless feline once said to haunt a house in Manchester.

Tales of witchcraft often say that live witches like to transform themselves into hares or rabbits, as well as cats, and may also take this form after death – like the hare that haunts Bolingbroke Castle in Lincolnshire where a witch once was imprisoned. In Cornwall, the ghost of a suicide (a girl) reappears as a white hare, and another Cornish girl who was seduced and betrayed returned after death to plague her lover in the form of a hare.

Ancient mystic beliefs have often seen the human soul in the shape of a bird, and so it is not surprising that many ghosts take this form. Sailors' superstitions especially see most seabirds as the ghosts of drowned sailors, and some of these – especially the so-called 'seven whistlers', which may be plovers – are invariably omens of disaster at sea. White birds appear to some aristocratic families as death omens – to the Oxenhams of Devon, the Wardours of Arundel, and, legend says, to the Bishop of Salisbury. (The birds that presage the death of the incumbent bishop were seen, according to Christina Hole, as recently as 1911.)

Alabama, USA, provides a tale of a jealous wife haunting her husband, after his remarriage, in the shape of a white dove. A human ghost that frightened the people of Coombe Valley, Staffordshire, was exorcised – but later reappeared in the less terrifying form of a bird. Other bird ghosts include a spectral black bird that haunted a church in Uxbridge, near London; a vicious ghost owl that attacked people in Russia in the late 19th century; and a 19th-century English bird ghost that heralded the death of several members of a woman's family.

Bears have shown up in a few good tales, and in some odd places: Worcester Cathedral supposedly has been haunted by a ghostly bear, as has the Tower of London. Somerset locals in the 16th century told of a fearsome headless bear accompanied by a reek of sulphur, while the same county in the next century produced the horrific vision of a bear with flaming eyes riding a huge, rolling, luminous wheel. A ghostly black bear that screams horribly has terrified travellers on a lonely road in the Alleghanies (USA).

Surrey boasts the ghost of a donkey, strangely coloured blue, while near Leeds was another spectral donkey with saucer eyes, called 'Padfoot', and known to be a death omen. White deer appear in many fairy tales and other legends, as elemental forest spirits, and a few have slipped over into ghost tales as well – like the white doe (said to be a witch's ghost) that haunted a hilltop in the west of England. Cattle emerge as revenants, too: a ghost bull in Shropshire, a great black bull seen in 1890 at a castle in County Clare, headless white calves in East Anglia, and the famous 'dun cow' of Warwickshire that appears to the Earl of Warwick, legend says, to herald a death in the family.

A much-used crossroads of the 19th century, near Oxford, was often the scene of the usual buryings of suicides and executed criminals (to keep the ghosts from returning), and many of the spectral beings held at the spot appeared as cattle or sheep. And a fairly modern tale from the north of England concerns a lamb whose ghostly bleating was heard in a house as a family death omen. Another omen of disaster was a spectral black pig, seen in Kiltrustan, Ireland, in 1918, before the outbreak of war; another black pig haunts a road in West Virginia, where it is often pursued but never caught.

Primitive jungle peoples have always infested their forests with ghostly wild animals – tigers, leopards, and so on – but these tend to be rather more like evil-natured spirits than revenants, and must be bypassed here. But we can include the spectre of a giant wolf that appeared to a Suffolk farmer long after wolves had been extinct in England. Then again, wolves have a special place of their own in folklore – as the terrifying supernatural creatures able to metamorphose from human to wolf, and called werewolves.

Still, the werewolf character in several Hollywood horror films was profferred as a revenant – a man murdered, buried with wolf's-bane, and so brought back to life as a shape-changer. And there is a little basis in folklore for this fiction. England's cruel King John, who in medieval legends was said to have been poisoned, was also said to have arisen again as a werewolf. Elliott O'Donnell mentions several tales of werewolves that were definitely supposed to be ghosts: one such in 19th-century Cumberland was done away with when some bones, both wolf and human, were found in a cave and burned. And Montague Summers relates a case of a giant ghost wolf with human (i.e. werewolf) eyes, seen in Wales in the 1880s, also exorcised when a wolf skull was found and destroyed.

Perhaps the modern film idea of a man dragged out of his coffin involuntarily, by some accidental magic – combining wolf's-bane with the full moon and so on – has some indirect connection with an assertion by the 16th-century mystic and magician Paracelsus: that people who live bestial lives will return after death in the shape of wild beasts. In any case, the horror-film notion, and other tales of werewolf revenants, can serve to bring us full circle – for the creatures are not insubstantial apparitions, but full-bodied and all too tangible, like the walking corpses with which we began.

Let Paracelsus's remark, then, serve as a final example to illustrate the major theme of this book: that mankind, throughout history, has fervently and consistently imposed an incredible variety of forms, human or otherwise, on the beings that he believes have returned from the dead.

Further Reading

Maurice Barbanell, *Spiritualism Today*, Herbert Jenkins, 1969

Dennis Bardens, *Ghosts and Hauntings*, Zeus Press, 1965

Hereward Carrington, *The Physical Phenomena of Spiritualism*, Chatto & Windus, 1907

Hereward Carrington and Nandor Fodor, *The Poltergeist down the Centuries*, Rider, 1953

Richard M. Dorson, *Jonathan Draws the Long Bow*, Harvard University Press, 1946

Eileen Garrett, *Many Voices*, Allen & Unwin, 1969

Douglas Hill and Pat Williams, *The Supernatural*, Aldus Books, 1965

Christina Hole, *Haunted England*, Batsford, 1940

Eric Maple, *The Realm of Ghosts*, Robert Hale, 1964

Elliott O'Donnell, *Ghosts Helpful and Harmful*, Rider, 1924

Elliott O'Donnell, *Animal Ghosts*, Rider, 1913

Frank Podmore, *Modern Spiritualism*, Methuen, 1902

W. B. Seabrook, *The Magic Island*, Harcourt, Brace & World, 1929

Sachaverell Sitwell, *Poltergeists*, Faber, 1940

Montague Summers, *The Vampire, His Kith and Kin*, Kegan Paul, 1928
    Vampire in Europe, Dutton, 1929

D. J. West, *Psychical Research Today*, Pelican, 1962

ABOUT THE AUTHOR

Douglas Hill is a Canadian who first came to Britain in 1959. Co-author with Pat Williams of *The Supernatural* (1965), his other books include *The Opening of the Canadian West* (1967), *Magic and Superstition* (1968), and *Regency London* in the London Weekend TV and Macdonald series *Discovering London* (1969). He has also edited four science-fiction and fantasy anthologies.

ACKNOWLEDGEMENTS

We are grateful to the following for permission to use copyright prints and photographs:
Camera Press London, 7; Michael Holford, 2; Mansell Collection, 10; National Film Archive, 4; Radio Times Hulton Picture Library, 3, 8; John Symonds, 9; Peter Underwood, 5.